6 $\frac{95}{}$

C+H

3-25-64 (64-11195)

Ancient Peoples and Places

SARDINIA

General Editor

DR. GLYN DANIEL

Ancient Peoples and Places

SARDINIA

Margaret Guido

77 PHOTOGRAPHS
56 LINE DRAWINGS
5 MAPS AND A
CHRONOLOGICAL TABLE

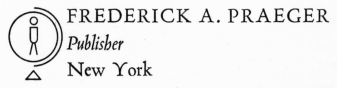

FREDERICK A. PRAEGER
Publisher
New York

THIS IS VOLUME THIRTY-FIVE IN THE SERIES
Ancient Peoples and Places
GENERAL EDITOR: DR. GLYN DANIEL

BOOKS THAT MATTER *Published in the United States of America
in 1964 by Frederick A. Praeger, Inc.,
Publisher, 64 University Place,
New York 3, N.Y.*
*© Margaret Guido 1963
Library of Congress Catalog Card Number: 64-11195
Printed in Great Britain by Hazell Watson & Viney Ltd.
Aylesbury, Bucks*

CONTENTS

ILLUSTRATIONS

Acknowledgements

I HAVE MUCH PLEASURE in thanking a number of friends for their interest and help during the preparation of this book. Firstly I want to thank Dr Glyn Daniel for kindly inviting me to write it, for it has opened up a new field of archaeological interest and acquainted me with a land of great and varied beauty. I am indebted to too many people to mention them all by name, but I have been particularly fortunate in being able to have long and profitable discussions with Dr Warwick Bray whose doctorate thesis on the Chambered Tombs of Sardinia was very generously put at my disposal, and to Signor Enrico Atzeni of Cagliari University, who has always, with a wide scholarly outlook, given me up-to-date information about his recent excavations, answered many queries, and provided me with valuable photographs.

I am equally grateful to my friends Professor and Mrs A. W. Lawrence, and Miss du Plat Taylor, who visited sites and museums in Sardinia with me. I wish to thank my friends Mrs Maxwell-Hyslop, Mr John Guthrie and Professor Stuart Piggott for kindly reading the typescript of this book, and for making comments which have led to its improvement. I am grateful, too, to the many firms, museum authorities and friends who have allowed me to use their photographs and field notes, and am especially indebted to Professor Christian Zervos who has allowed me to reproduce 15 photographs from his book *La Civilisation de la Sardaigne . . .*, and to Ing. Teodoro Cima for having sent me several books which would otherwise have escaped my notice.

The book has greatly profited from the excellent drawings of Mrs Scott and Mr Shelley, and of Signori Lazzarini and Giocastro of the Soprintendenza alle Antichità at Syracuse. I would like to thank them all.

13

Acknowledgements

I gratefully acknowledge, too, the help and friendliness that everyone in Sardinia accorded me, from University professors and Museum authorities to shepherds and small boys who have taken me across country to visit monuments in the field.

Lastly I wish to thank the staff of Thames & Hudson for their kind and efficient co-operation at all stages of the book's production.

M. G.

Introduction

SARDINIA IS A LAND of contrasts, of mountains and plains, barren rocks and stagnant marshes; lush as the English countryside in spring, baked and torpid as the South American pampas in summer; the lowlands of the south and west open to trade and new ideas, even if the nature of the people never really welcomed either, and the uplands proudly conservative and steeped in tradition – its inhabitants unafraid of isolation and fighting to the last to remain free.

This conservatism, this hostility to change explains a great deal in Sardinian prehistory. It partly explains the curious fact that even today, over much of the island it is the prehistoric period rather than the present which makes the greater impact. Another contributory explanation for this fact lies in the undeveloped character of the island: undeveloped and unexploited through centuries of poverty, and with a climate where malaria has only been stamped out within living memory. On all sides, where woods are not too dense, the rocky skyline is broken by remains of tombs, fortresses, and above all the tower-like nuraghi (see Chapter IV), over 6,500 of them scattered over the countryside which for miles on end may be forest, rock-strewn scrub, or sheep pastures interspersed with coppices, without a sign of the handiwork of modern times.

Plate I

All these contrasts in the physiognomy of the island might lead one to imagine that the various prehistoric groups inhabiting Sardinia were fragmented and regionally distinct, each adapted to the way of life required by its environment, and to a certain extent this is true; but only at the dawn of its prehistory. Gradually the various elements merged to make a homogeneous whole by the time of the so-called Nuragic culture which prevailed for a millennium or more, from approximately 1400 to 300 BC. Political unity of course there was not, but an underlying cultural unity grew up, within the general framework of which local strife, warfare, vendettas, as well as local dialects, crafts and customs have left their evidence in the archaeological record. It is this record that concerns us here.

We shall begin with an account of the land itself, a land which has been more hostile to change and more proudly individual than perhaps any other part of Europe, and where the physical type and even the character of its present inhabitants still share much with those of their prehistoric forebears. We shall then follow the arrival of the earliest settlers in the Neolithic period (third millennium BC) and in the Eneolithic or Copper age when groups from both the east and west Mediterranean settled on the coast. In the Bronze Age we see a period of consolidation working towards the slow development of the long Nuragic period, after the earliest nuraghi were built in the mid second millennium. By the early first millennium, when this culture was reaching full maturity, the first Phoenician prospectors were already probing the resources of the island, and cultural exchanges both with them and their warlike Punic (Carthaginian) successors temporarily enriched the indigenous civilisation. From the sixth century BC until the arrival of the Romans in the third century BC and even later, the story is of intermittent bloodshed, raids and reprisals – the lowlands under the domination of Carthage and enjoying a certain prosperity; the uplands unconquered and unchanged. We see the increasing tiredness of the lingering Nuragic culture, and its final subjugation, but never extinction, by the Romans.

Many scholars have worked to reconstruct Sardinia's prehistory and early history; far too many for more than a few to be mentioned here. La Marmora in the early nineteenth century was the first to make a serious investigation, and his field work led to the two volumes of his *Voyage en Sardaigne* (1839), which provide us with a fascinating account of many monuments now wholly or partially destroyed. This led to an ever-increasing interest which has reached its crescendo in the splendid annual publication of *Studi Sardi*. But before the foundation of this in 1934 much patient research of a high quality was carried out by others, notably Pinza, Pais and Patroni, whose work, though now largely superseded, was of high value in its time. The dominant name in Sardinian studies is that of Antonio Taramelli, whose numerous reports, mostly in *Monumenti Antichi* and *Notizie degli Scavi* over many years, have provided the primary sources for so much that we know today, admirably supplemented by the fieldwork of Duncan Mackenzie. More recently a classic study, *La Sardegna Nuragica* (1950) was written by Prof. M. Pallottino; a small but invaluable work which, though now a little out of date, remains a most valuable contribution well deserving a revised edition. In recent years again, the various studies and excavations of Prof. Giovanni Lilliu are outstanding: indeed this book owes more to the last-mentioned scholars for their interpretations of Sardinian prehistory than could possibly be acknowledged in the text. Lilliu's most recent book on Sardinian prehistory, *La Civiltà dei Sardi* was published while this book was in the press.

Readers seeking a full bibliography (though only up to 1953) should turn to Christian Zervos's volume *La Civilisation de la Sardaigne* ... (1954) which also contains a magnificent collection of photographs, some of which, by kind consent of the author, are reproduced here. The most recent book on Punic Sardinia is *Sardegna Punica* (1961) by Gennaro Pesce.

Sardinia's prehistory is still far from clear, but its main framework is established to some extent, and the detail will be added when more fieldwork, and above all excavations with recorded stratigraphy, have been carried out. The nature of much of the terrain retards and complicates field researches, and it should be remembered that it is still often necessary to go miles on horseback or on foot to visit sites hidden among rocks or forest, overgrown and almost indistinguishable. We are still near to the times when Duncan Mackenzie could give no better point of reference than '3 hours south-west of Bultei'. For these reasons distribution maps of Sardinian antiquities are far from complete, though forest fires, land development, and chance discoveries by shepherds or road builders are daily adding to the archaeological record. The prime need, however, lies in the excavation of stratified sites, with which we are so ill provided today.

The island is now divided into two administrative provinces, one at Cagliari and the other at Sassari (which includes the province of Nuoro), each with its *Soprintendenza alle Antichità*, under whose aegis monuments are recorded, restored or excavated, and preserved from unauthorised excavation which activity still, inevitably, takes place. On the whole, however, the Sardinians are anxious to preserve vestiges of their past, in which they take a deep and justifiable pride, feeling themselves to be inheritors of a history which does not closely resemble that of any other part of Europe, and from whose vivid record we can reconstruct at least some aspects of the life and thought of the people.

CHRONOLOGICAL
TABLE

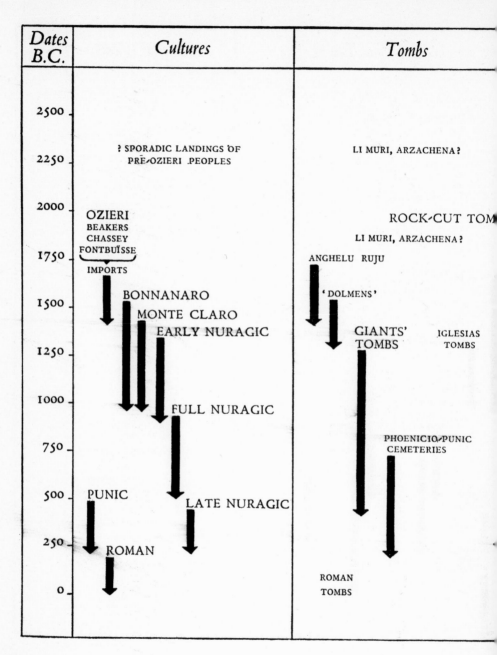

Dates B.C.	Cultures	Tombs

2500

2250 — ? SPORADIC LANDINGS OF PRE-OZIERI PEOPLES   LI MURI, ARZACHENA?

2000 — OZIERI   ROCK-CUT TOM
BEAKERS
CHASSEY   LI MURI, ARZACHENA?
FONTBUÏSSE
1750 —   ANGHELU RUJU
IMPORTS

BONNANARO   'DOLMENS'
1500 —
MONTE CLARO

EARLY NURAGIC   GIANTS'   IGLESIAS
TOMBS   TOMBS
1250 —

1000 — FULL NURAGIC

750 —   PHOENICIO-PUNIC
CEMETERIES

500 — PUNIC   LATE NURAGIC

250 — ROMAN

ROMAN
0 — TOMBS

Buildings and Towns	Historical Events	Dates B.C.
		2500
	? SPORADIC CONTACTS WITH EAST MEDITERRANEAN CULMINATING IN	2250
	ARRIVAL OF E. MEDITERRANEAN-INSPIRED OZIERI CULTURE	2000
OPEN SETTLEMENTS	CONTACTS WITH PYRENEES, S. FRANCE AND WITH MALTA, ITALY, CORSICA ETC.	1750
ARLY VILLAGES		
	PERIOD OF CONSOLIDATION AND RELATIVE ISOLATION	1500
MONTE D'ACCODDI SA CORONA VILLAGRECA		
ARCHAIC NURAGHI		1250
	(? arrival of Shardana)	
? (SOME GALLERY NURAGHI)		1000
EVOLVED NURAGHI { NORA, SULCIS, KARALIS, AND THARROS founded by Phoenicians	PHOENICIAN SETTLEMENTS FOUNDED	
GALLERY NURAGHI WELL TEMPLES SANCTUARIES AND NURAGIC VILLAGES	Trade with Etruria, Cyprus and Spain, etc.	750
SACRED WELLS	Phocaean colony at Olbia?	
PUNIC TOWNS	CARTHAGINIAN INVASION C. 510	500
		250
PUNICO-ROMAN BUILDINGS	238 ROMAN OCCUPATION 177 LAST SERIOUS NATIVE STAND	
		0

CHAPTER I

The Setting

THE LAND AND ITS RESOURCES

SARDINIA OCCUPIES, with Corsica, a central position in the western Mediterranean. Sicily, Malta, North Africa, southern France, Spain and the Balearics were all within reasonable sailing distance by the early second millennium, when improved navigation led to the opening up of the sea, ways. To the north the straits of Bonifacio, a narrow but current,swept channel, separates Sardinia from Corsica, while near,by Elba in turn provides a convenient stepping,stone between Corsica and the Italian mainland.

Fig. 1

A glance at the map would suggest that early navigators sailing to or from Sardinia had to remain long out of sight of land, but this is not so, owing to the high peaks which were visible from considerable distances. As Cary has written, 'Before the coast of France disappears from his view, a seaman will descry the tall shoulder of Mt Cinto in north,west Corsica; with Sardinia still in sight he will make out the islands that fringe the northern coast of Tunisia.' It is, more, over, possible on clear winter days to stand at Punta Sebèra near Teulada on the south,west coast of Sardinia, and glimpse the northern tip of Africa.

Sardinia is somewhat larger than Corsica, and measures about 150 miles from north to south, and 75 miles from east to west at its widest point. So close are the two islands that it is no surprise to find that geologically Sardinia is a continuation of Corsica. Many of its rocks are extremely ancient and metal, bearing due to the mineralisation of Palaeozoic rocks, and these ores served to attract early settlers. The geological forma, tion is, however, so heterogeneous in character that a clear

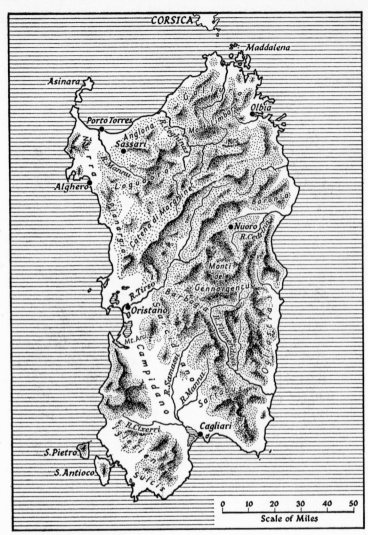

CORSICA

Maddalena

Asinara

Porto Torres
Anglona
Sassari

Olbia

Alghero

Logudoro

Catena di Marghine

Nuoro
R.Ced

Monti del
Gennargentu

R.Tirso

Oristano

Mt.Arci

Campidano

R.Mannu

R.Cixerri

Cagliari

S.Pietro

S.Antioco

Sulcis

| 0 | 10 | 20 | 30 | 40 | 50 |
Scale of Miles

Fig. 1. Relief map of Sardinia

description is difficult. The simplified map on the opposite
page will facilitate an understanding of the island's terrain.

Most of Sardinia is composed of mountains and upland
plateaux, often of granite and intersected by small torrents,

Fig. 2

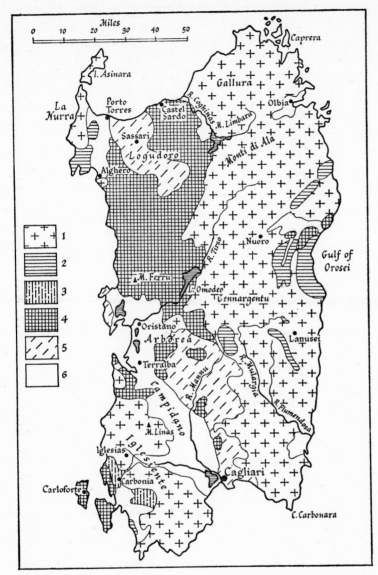

Fig. 2. Geological map of Sardinia showing principal formations. (1) Ancient Hercynian horsts; (2) Mesozoic limestones; (3) Eocene rocks; (4) Volcanic rocks; (5) Miocene marls and clays; (6) Quaternary deposits and recent alluvium. (After Walker)

most of which dry up in the summer months. Though little navigable, these must nevertheless have served as rough routes in prehistoric times; up their dried, stony beds the early herds, men could drive their flocks more easily than through the uncleared forests, while at certain seasons the pools lingering among the rocks served not only to water their flocks but to attract the wild animals to drink, and so to fall an easy prey to the hunters.

Most of the high land lies to the east of the island, its highest and most inaccessible region being the wild bare peaks of the Gennargentu, rising to little more than 5,000 feet. For the rest, few of the uplands exceed 3,000 feet, but the rocks com, posing them are most varied: some are karstic limestone, some granite, others trachite or basalt. Forests of oak, chestnut or cork trees once covered most of these massifs but are now only extensive in the Gallura and in the Gennargentu. The east side of the island, from the Gallura in the north,east almost as far as the south coast, is mostly granite, wild boulder,strewn land often thick with lentisk or cistus. It has sharp, craggy summits and wide valleys. The rocks are often weathered into fantastic shapes, especially in the Gallura, which has a character all its own, and the vegetation is frequently patchy *macchia* dotted with oaks scattered over pasture or arable which is poorly watered.

Plate 1

A somewhat similar formation is found in the south,west, in the Iglesiente: here again the mountains are granite and there are sedimentary and metamorphic rocks often rich with iron ore and nickel. This is the main mining area of present, day Sardinia. Again, in the north,west tip of the island, in the Nurra, a great deal of metalliferous rock is found, this time containing lead and copper. Most of these rocks are imperme, able, and the characteristic features of the areas where they occur are widespread erosion and flooding, with frequent marshes even on high land.

From Cagliari in the south up to beyond the Gulf of Oristano and the mouth of the island's biggest river, the Tirso, runs an undulating strip of country known as the Campidano, dominated towards its northern end by Monte Arci, an extinct volcano whose slopes are still strewn with obsidian, or volcanic glass, so much prized by prehistoric man. The Campidano is low, gently rolling land, formed of alluvial deposits that are easy to cultivate. This is the most tractable part of all Sardinia, and must always have provided easy access to the north from the natural harbours of Cagliari. To the west of it lies the Iglesiente and its mountains: to north-east of it runs a parallel strip of higher land, mostly limestone eroded into a series of low plateaux, or cultivable marls: beyond this again lies the Barbagia running up north-eastwards to the oak and chestnut woods and bare peaks of the Gennargentu. Continuing northwards from the Campidano an extensive tract of lava and tufa leads into the limestone rocks of the Sassari district, one of the most extensively occupied parts of the island in prehistoric times.

Sardinia's east coast is somewhat forbidding and difficult of access, the coastal strip being narrow and backed by forest land. Pausanias (*Book X*, 17) describes it as follows: 'The northern part of the island and that towards the mainland of Italy consist of an unbroken chain of impassable mountains. And if you sail along the coast you will find no anchorage on this side of the island, while violent but irregular gusts of wind sweep down to the sea from the tops of the mountains.' Both traders and invaders found their easiest entry from the south, west or north-west. These coasts are rich in bays, lagoons and marshy land, good for fishing and wild-fowling; natural harbours abound, particularly little sandy inlets known as *cale* or *calette*, large enough to protect small boats and offering easy access into what is here a less thickly wooded hinterland.

At first sight it would seem from the few rivers which do not dry up in the hot months that early settlers must have had difficulty in finding an adequate water-supply. But hot and cold springs are found all over the island, and that these were highly prized is shown by the number of them which were, in Nuragic times at least, regarded as sacred. The Tirso river generally runs throughout the year, as do also the small but prehistorically important Mannu river in the north-west, the Flumendosa and several others. In the north-west too near Porto Ferro, is the Lago di Barazza, a small fresh-water lake. The two big lakes, Coghinas and Omodeo, were made artificially in recent years.

We have already mentioned some of the natural resources of Sardinia, but there are others which attracted early settlers and which in the course of time came to be exploited. We have spoken of Monte Arci with its obsidian which can be chipped and pressure-flaked into fine implements: this would have had a still greater and not merely local importance, had it not been for the discovery in the Lipari islands of an even richer supply which drew prospectors from the other end of the Mediter-ranean. We have also spoken of the metal ores, lead, antimony, zinc, nickel, iron, copper and silver, found in Sardinian rocks, and to these resources should be added coral near Alghero and steatite near Orani. Cassiterite also occurs, but may not have been discovered till after the Nuragic period. Previously, tin may have been imported from Iberia or Tuscany. Sardinian silver was mainly exported by Phoenician traders, as is attested by Diodorus Siculus. But many of these metals were worked from an early period, as the moulds and crucibles, and the foundries in nuragic settlements all testify.

By Strabo's time (1st BC–1st AD) corn was cultivated ex-tensively and was one of the chief commodities. Strabo des-cribes Sardinia as a 'rugged and wild country, but a large part contains much fertile land, rich in all kinds of produce, and most specially in corn.' He was thinking most probably of the Campidano and the lower, western parts of the island, to this day its main granary, whereas the uplands are chiefly sheep pastures and woods. Diodorus Siculus mentions the island's fruits as one of its riches.

Sardinia must also have been abundant in game and various kinds of animal products, including skins. The fauna here is different from that of Corsica, though certain animals, for instance the elsewhere extinct mouflon (*Ovis musimon*) is still common to both. In ancient times, before the island was inhabited by man, antelope, deer, wild boar, dwarf elephants, bears, monkeys, wild dogs and crocodiles abounded, as well as many species of birds. It has not been definitely established whether the horse (*Equus caballus*) was also indigenous, or whether it was introduced by Semitic peoples. Some of these animals survived long enough to leave evidence in the archaeo-logical record. Gradually many species became extinct, and the systematic clearing of the forests and woods by the Car-thaginians drove many of the surviving ones into the mountains. Oxen and pigs were introduced relatively late, and seals still breed in the coastal caves near Cala Gonone and elsewhere.

This, then, is the early scene: a land hard to cultivate, heavily forested and swarming with wild animals, difficult of access except from Corsica, owing to the primitive state of navigation before the late third or early second millennium BC. It is therefore no surprise to find that the archaeological record suggests little occupation before that time.

LITERARY AND LINGUISTIC EVIDENCE

The component elements of the proto-Sardinian population will perhaps, in time, be more easily distinguishable from archaeological than from linguistic or literary data. As far as the linguistic evidence is concerned, all we can say is that there are a number of words in the existing dialects, or in those known from earlier documents, particularly names of natural features like rivers, mountains, etc., which have no origin in the Greek, Latin or Punic languages, and they must presumably belong to an earlier age. This is all the more probable as they are distributed over the whole island, and are not limited to areas of foreign occupation; they may, in fact, be vestiges of the language commonly spoken in the period of the Nuragic culture.

The roots of these dialects do not seem to match up with either Semitic or Indo-European languages, but may belong to an underlying pre-Indo-European substratum widely spread over the Mediterranean, more particularly in the western and central parts. They are noticeably divergent from the non-Indo-European language of the Italian mainland; a circum-stance that supports the archaeological record of the island which at no time closely conforms with that of the mainland. The Sardinian dialects also show analogies with both Basque and the North African Libyan languages, and even with those of the Balkan and Danubian areas, though here the resemblances are more distant.

The strongest correspondences lie with Iberia. Sardinia had cultural contacts both with Spain, particularly Catalonia, and the Balearics by the second millennium BC. The legendary foundation of Nora in Sardinia by an Iberian chief Norax from Tartessos, may be symbolic of the proto-Iberian in-fluences on the island from Beaker times onwards. The name Nora is, in fact, related to many personal and place names in North Africa, Spain and Sardinia, and may contain the same root as the word 'nuraghe'. In this connection it is interesting to note that the early name of Minorca was Nura.

Pausanias speaks of the transfer of Spanish mercenaries to Sardinia at about the time of the foundation of Nora, evidently thinking that this took place at the time of the Carthaginians.

In fact he claims that some Iberians and Libyans deserted from the invading army and set up a resistance movement. These deserters were known as Balaroi, which may possibly be the name of the inhabitants of the Balearics, or may simply mean 'refugees'. An alternative explanation for the similarity between the Sardinian and Balearic name may be that some people of the Sardinian group known as the Balares (or Balari) settled in the Balearics before the time of the Carthaginian invasion, and gave their name to the islands. We cannot be sure to what period the Norax legend relates, but in any case connections between Sardinia and Iberia and the Balearics existed, directly or indirectly, from the second millennium and increased during the first millennium B C. In Cagliari there are three Iberian inscriptions of the last centuries B C.

The African element in the language may have come with a definite transfer of people from Libya to Sardinia at a very early date, but so far this has not been archaeologically supported in spite of the legends, and it must be remembered that Punicised Libyans must have been brought to the island at the time of the Carthaginian conquest.

As one might expect from its proximity, there are also elements in common with Corsica. Whether these should be referred to the Copper Age when Corsica and Gallura had many cultural contacts, or whether they are due to later immigrations across the Straits of Bonifacio, it is impossible to say. The early writers refer to people known as 'Corsi', perhaps descendants of the Corsican settlers in the Gallura.

Thus, superimposed on the original population, there were foreign elements due to reciprocal trade exchanges along established sea routes which would, from time to time, bring small groups of settlers from the nearer shores. In the western Mediterranean cultural cohesion was facilitated by the sea currents and the relative proximity of the lands sharing a basically similar language; contacts with the east, though persistent, were more difficult and intermittent, and must largely have been brought about by coastal trade and sporadic landings of prospectors. There must also have been many purely accidental arrivals of boats blown off course.

At the time of the first historical sources and the earliest legends, that is, at the time of the Carthaginian and Roman occupations, the ethnical elements were twofold: the agricul/tural and trading peoples of the western and southern lowlands and coasts, in touch with the colonists, and the more backward pastoral peoples living in the mountainous areas of the eastern part of the island. There may also have been a small number of Greeks, if some scholars are right in thinking that Olbia was at one time a Greek port. How early this division became apparent is not known. Linguistically, as has been said, there is a strong suggestion of uniformity all over the island at an early date. In the oriental documents of the second millennium, as well as in the Phoenician inscriptions at Nora and the earliest Greek sources, the term 'Sardi' was used to denote the inhabitants of the island, or at least certain elements in the population: we do not know which.

Plate 69

Our only sources of information are derived from the outside world, from Greeks, Romans and Carthaginians visiting the island or hearing about it from sailors. Most of the classical sources, at least the early ones, are so speculative or politically biased that they are of little value; and to add to the difficulties, the original text has often been lost and the later versions are distorted or rewritten.

In the fifth century B C Herodotus writes of plans for colonis/ing Sardinia with Ionians; a century later Aristotle mentions the tombs dedicated to heroes in Sardinia, and subsequently we hear more of these from Solinus and Ptolemy who tell us that the tomb of Iolaus was venerated in a sanctuary, and that Sardus had a temple called after him, the Temple of Sardus Pater, in the south/west of the island. In the *Odyssey* there is a reference to the sardonic smile of Odysseus, but its connection with Sardinia is by no means established. Nor can the peoples known as the Shardana in Egyptian sources of the fourteenth–twelfth centuries B C be definitely identified with the Sardinians; but this will be discussed later. From the early references we learn of an originally deserted island, only inhabited by enormous birds. Various immigrants and colonisers, often identified with heroes, include the Libyans under Sardus, the Iberians under Norax, Thespians under Iolaus, the companion of Herakles, and many others from the Greek world. Naturally it was in the Greek interest to claim their own colonisation of Sardinia in order to substantiate their rightful possession when it was disputed – successfully – by the Carthaginians.

Historical events are only glimpsed at first, but gradually they become more and more detailed in Hellenistic times and later. Strabo hints that the Sardinians were Tyrrhenians, but this reference may hark back to the earlier Sardinian-Etruscan connections, or it may simply mean that they were western people. The same writer speaks of the Sardinians from the mountains raiding the Etruscan shores. Others mention the development of agriculture, and the great size of the architectural monuments made 'with a primitive Greek technique': evidently these were the nuraghi whose *tholos*-type roofing was reminiscent of the great tombs of the Mycenaean world. Some accounts claim that these buildings were made by Daedalus who came to Sardinia from Crete. Others lament the barbarisation of the island as being due to Carthaginian settlement; but as we have stressed, many of the Greek writers say derogatory things of their rivals, and cannot be taken too seriously.

By Hellenistic times, and later, from Diodorus Siculus, Pliny, Pausanias, Solinus and others, we learn far more, and often in considerable detail. Diodorus and Polybius write of the Phoenician and Carthaginian colonisation, and by the

Plate 32

time of the Roman military expeditions, some accounts are full and detailed.

From the historians we also learn something of the island tribes. Ptolemy gives a list of names but makes no distinction between the peoples of the mountains and those of the low-lands. We hear from other sources of *Corsi* (probably in the north and of Corsican origin) and of *Iliei* or *Balari* in the mountains. Strabo calls all these peoples *Iolaei* and subdivides them into four groups known as *Paratoi* (or *Taratoi*), *Sassinatoi*, *Balaroi* and *Achonites*. In Latin inscriptions the following tribes are mentioned, and some of them coincide with the ethnical groups mentioned by Ptolemy:

Nurr(enses) in the Nuoro district.
Gallilenses in the Barbagia.
Rubrenses in the Ogliastra (east of the Gennargentu).
Cusin(itani ?) and *Celes(itani* ?) in the Gennargentu.
Giddilitani and *Uddaharitani* near Bosa, to the west.
Moltamonenses and *Semelitenses* on the borders of Cagliari and the Campidano.

Naturally the boundaries between these tribes were never fixed and may have fluctuated considerably. Of all those known to the ancient world, perhaps the *Balari* were the most powerful; they were still known by repute in Roman times. We have already drawn attention to Pausanias's claim that they were originally auxiliaries who had defected from the Carthaginian army, and this is by no means impossible. These people seem to have occupied the uplands near Budduso and Bitti and possibly parts of the Gallura as well, but the information at our disposal is tantalisingly scarce, and presents a ready pitfall for those searching to equate tribal with topographical names.

Several names for the island itself have come down to us. Herodotus speaks of 'Sardo, the greatest of the isles of the sea.' Pausanias wrote: 'What the ancient name was that the natives gave it I do not know, but those of the Greeks who sailed there to trade called it *Ichnussa* because the shape of the island is very like a man's footprint (*ichnos*).' Other versions include *Sandaliotis* (sandal) and the originally Latin, present name of *Sardinia*. Shardan is the name given to Sardinia on the Phoenician inscription from Nora. Its date is disputed but it is likely to belong to the eighth century B C or thereabouts.

CHAPTER II

Earliest Settlers

SOME EARLY SITES

THE PREHISTORIC SETTLEMENT of Sardinia, and Corsica as far as we know, did not begin until relatively late in comparison with Sicily, Italy and other mainland parts of the Continent. In fact, while Upper Palaeolithic man crossed the Straits of Messina to reach Sicily, Sardinia evidently lay beyond the range of the simple craft of the period, and was not apparently occupied until the third millennium or the dawn of the second millennium BC.

In the next chapters we shall examine the evidence for this earliest settlement in the Copper Age when the Ozieri culture was introduced from the Eastern Mediterranean only shortly before contacts were established with south-west France and perhaps Spain. It may be that previously small boatloads of people, drifting off course, made occasional landings in Neolithic times. But as yet evidence for this is meagre, and the few sites which may prove to be earlier than the Ozieri culture cannot be placed for certain in their chronological order, owing to the lack of closely comparable material from elsewhere in the Mediterranean. The so-called 'Venus' from the S'Adde rock-shelter at Macomer, discussed on page 47, may prove to be earlier than the Ozieri culture, though this is improbable.

Plates 7–9

The most puzzling site is, perhaps, that of Li Muri near Arzachena in the Gallura. There, about twenty years ago, excavations were made in a group of stone cist graves. These cists, which are surrounded by contiguous circular platforms (or, less probably, denuded cairns) and are associated with standing stones, were placed on alluvial sand in a countryside

Fig. 3

which is one of the strangest and most beautiful in Sardinia: granite rocks weathered to fantastic shapes and rich in natural caves and cavities, some of which have also been excavated.

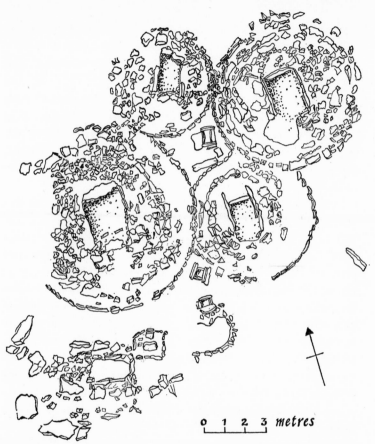

Fig. 3. Complex of cairns, cists and standing stones at Li Muri, Arzachena. (After Puglisi)

Excavations have recently been resumed in this district with the aim of elucidating both the chronological and cultural setting of Li Muri, which, in spite of distinctive grave goods, still remains something of a mystery, being unique in the island. That the site is one of the earliest megalithic monuments in Sardinia cannot, however, be denied.

Each of the five cairns composing the group contained a central rectangular cist made of upright slabs, once probably covered. Around each was a series of concentric rings of lower stones, sometimes as many as five rings. Associated with these tombs were three small cists, perhaps for offerings, and at least four standing stones which may have had a commemorative or religious significance. One of them stood in a square enclosure of upright slabs.

The finds all came from the central cists, only one of which contained the remains of a skeleton. The pottery was roughly made and reddish in colour, but too fragmentary to reveal the original forms. There were also a number of obsidian and *Fig. 4* flint flakes. *Tomb I* contained a fine steatite cup with footring and spool handles, an axe-amulet, a thick, polished axe perhaps of serpentine, part of a perforated spherical mace-head, another triangular polished one, fragments of long flint knives, a necklace of stone beads, discoidal, spherical or elongated in shape, a bone point, and pottery. *Tomb 2* contained a triangular flat axe, a spherical mace-head with hour-glass perforation, and some stone beads. *Tomb 3* was empty, and *Tomb 4* pro-duced four triangular greenstone axes, five perforated spherical mace-heads, and a necklace of stone beads. From *Tomb 5* came two fragments of long flint knives, and stone beads. Red ochre was also discovered in some of the cists.

At the time of publication, Puglisi thought that both the finds and the type of tomb pointed to an inspiration from Sicily or southern Italy in the Neolithic or Copper Age. But in fact there is nothing very closely comparable in Sicily, and the Apulian cists of the 'Murge' near Bari, while closely com-parable for their construction with concentric rings of stones around a central cist, have not produced any dateable finds, though not far away, near Bitonto, some rather different but

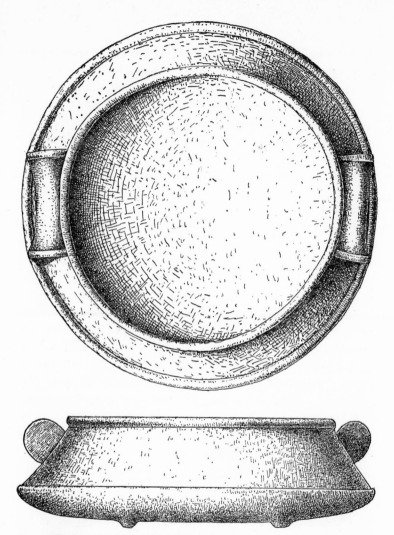

Fig. 4. The steatite bowl from Li Muri, Arzachena. 1 : 1

probably related graves seem to belong to the Early Iron Age. The tomb type is found in individual examples in a bell-beaker context in Catalonia, at Bressol de la Mare de Déu (Correá) and Serrat dels Quadrats (Muntant), and recently an even more comparable tomb has been discovered at La Boussière, Cabasse (Var). Here in a round cairn or platform of stones was a square cist containing stone beads. The tomb was dated by Carbon 14 analysis to about 2025±130 B C.

Fig. 4
However, at least one object found at Li Muri suggests East Mediterranean inspiration; this is the steatite bowl, the stone of which may be of Cretan origin.

On Levkas off the west coast of mainland Greece, Dörp-feld found a somewhat similar group of round platforms (or perhaps denuded cairns) surrounding cists. These produced characteristic Early Helladic pottery, while what seem to be secondary pyres on the platforms included rather later objects of the early second millennium. We should also note some cist graves of Cycladic type at Hagios Kosmas in Attica, several centuries earlier than the Levkas tombs. They contained Cycladic stone idols, and a stone platter with spool handles rather like that from Li Muri. Other analogies for the steatite bowl, though not very close, can be found from Crete in the proto-Minoan period, and others from the Fourth Dynasty in Egypt. Stone bowls are also known from the Cyclades, and Childe has suggested that they may represent a Nilotic tendency like the fish emblems on the North Cycladic boats. One should also remember the close resemblance between the Li Muri bowl and the Diana style pottery bowls in Lipari.

Lilliu has quoted parallels for the stone beads from Mochlos (E.M.II) and for the so-called mace-heads, from Knossos as well as Anatolia and Egypt.

Further excavations may help us to date these tombs. At the moment we must either regard Li Muri as belonging to a local facies of the Copper Age, contemporary with the Ozieri culture, early in the second millennium (in which case the steatite bowl remains a mystery), or we must imagine a small group of East Mediterranean people landing in the Gallura several centuries earlier, in the third millennium B.C.

Pottery similar to that from Li Muri came from the rock shelter of Le Casacce in the same district, and not far away some stone circles have been excavated and found to contain stone cists or a rough stela in the centre. Some of these circles have a well made entrance and look like hut foundations, but the excavator regards them as funerary or cult sites.

THE OZIERI CULTURE AND THE ROCK⁄CUT TOMBS

The pottery which has more recently been recognised as typical of the main group of Copper Age settlers in Sardinia was first found on a large scale in the cave of San Michele just outside Ozieri, excavated in 1915. In plan it is a long, irregular natural cavern in the karstic limestone, opening from a steep drop of about 20 feet into a main chamber beyond which was another, smaller one and a labyrinth of minor bifurcations and crannies.

The pottery found unstratified in this cave was for the most part finely decorated, and there was little or no occupation refuse. A human skull and some long bones were found, as well as flint knives, an obsidian core, a small polished green⁄stone axe⁄amulet, pebbles foreign to the district, and a long rounded bone pin or spatula. Later investigations in 1949 produced a number of other objects, some probably intrusive, including ochre, a spindle⁄whorl, bone points, and an in⁄teresting fragment of a limestone pebble incised on both faces with what appear to be anthropomorphic designs. A rather similar pebble was found on the surface in the pre⁄nuragic village of Puisteris, Mogoro. A little Bonnanaro ware was also present. This type of pottery is discussed below (page 68).

Fig. 5

The extremely difficult access to this cave and the fact that it had been carefully blocked with two tall cylindrical granite slabs, brought from a distance, each about 6 feet in height, and possibly originally forming one huge slab, lead one to suppose that the cave housed one or more burials of exceptional importance, regarded with veneration, and never intended to be disturbed. A magico-religious significance may also be attached to the axe-amulet and to the incised pebble which, though incomplete, recalls some of the 'goddess' figures widely spread over the Mediterranean at the time.

Fig. 16

The pottery provides a type series for the Ozieri culture which is now known from many other Sardinian sites, from other caves, from open villages, and above all from the rock-cut or 'domus de gianus' tombs. It is therefore convenient here to describe the characteristics of this pottery in its widest variety, not limiting ourselves only to the cave of San Michele.

The decorated Ozieri pottery was recently studied by Audibert who divided it into two groups on the basis of its decorative style. On further consideration such a division seems unwarranted, and it can all be treated together. This pottery is quite unlike anything else in Sardinia or elsewhere, and can easily be recognised. The standard both of potting and of decoration often reaches extreme competence. The surface is polished or burnished, and may have a slip, or be 'painted' with stripes of red ochre. Glossy black (*nero-lucido*) and glossy coral red wares are common, and sometimes the paste is pale buff in colour, and carries a light glossy slip. The larger pots are often undecorated or have only a notched cordon, but the smaller ones are skilfully decorated with both rectilinear and curvilinear designs: zigzags, hatched triangles, arcs, semicircles, concentric festoons, star-like patterns generally incised or impressed on the clay before firing, and often accentuated with red or white filling. Many of the designs combine hatched curvilinear zones contrasting with blank circles or spaces, the two elements being equally important to the effect obtained. Sometimes the pottery may be scratched after firing, or even decorated with shell-edge impressions, and sometimes may be grooved or channelled. At the village site of San Gemiliano

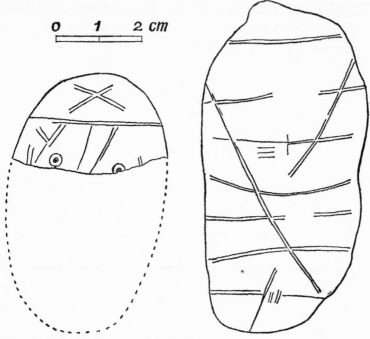

0   1   2 cm

Fig. 5. Incised pebbles from S. Michele di Ozieri (left) and Puisteris (Mogoro)

an unusual decoration of contrasting colour was achieved by first putting on a yellowish slip, and then covering the un‑decorated parts of the pot with a red slip.

The shapes are mostly carinated, though hemispherical bowls, often decorated on the lower part, are also common; some of these were, perhaps, lids. Straight‑sided 'flower‑pot' forms (*pyxides*) are frequently found, often ornamented with filled designs. Tripods are usually made of plain ware, and their feet are often concave on the outer side. The most charac‑teristic handles are the 'tunnel handles' of Peu Richard (France) and Tarxien (Malta) affinities. Sometimes there are string‑holes on the carination, and the bases are normally flat, occasionally convex or with little feet.

Plates 2, 3 and 4

43

This Ozieri ware has so far largely been found in the better explored western half of Sardinia, particularly in the Campi-dano and in the less mountainous parts of the island. It is also common in the Sassari-Alghero region and has recently been reported from the Gallura and near Dorgali and Nuoro. Together with it in the various caves, villages and rock-cut tombs, querns and grain-rubbers have been found and show that the Ozieri people were cultivating grain, and the animals which they hunted or domesticated included rabbits, hares, deer, oxen, pigs, wild boar, horses, sheep, dogs, foxes and goats. They also, no doubt, fished in the lagoons and ate limpets and other shellfish. Spindle-whorls and loom weights indicate their knowledge of weaving, and building and tree-felling can be inferred from the numerous stone axes often made of carefully selected hard stones such as basalt, nephrite or porphyrite, sometimes polished. Polished stone mace-heads also seem to belong to this culture.

The obsidian scattered over the slopes of Monte Arci was commonly used, both the opaque and translucent varieties, for making scrapers, knives, burins and arrowheads, and large quantities of flakes which often show secondary working on one face. The arrowheads, some of which may have been imported, are leaf-shaped and tanged, or barbed and tanged with pressure-flaking on both surfaces. Certainly the import-ance of obsidian to a people with little if any knowledge of metal-working, cannot be over-emphasised.

Many of the finer implements were made of flint, possibly an even more prized substance. Very long trapeze-sectioned blades sometimes reach over 20 cm. in length, and have slight re-touching along the cutting edges or at the ends. The flint arrowheads are normally tanged, and there are no hollow-based ones either of flint or obsidian.

Religion evidently played an important part in the lives of these people. The sacred site of Monte D'Accoddi (see p. 59),

Plates 19, 20

the decorations incised or carved on the tombs and the numerous statuette-idols all reveal local versions of religious concepts from various parts of the Eastern Mediterranean. More than 20 small idols have been discovered in Sardinia, and though these are by no means identical with the Cycladic ones, they must certainly have ultimately stemmed from them or from the same ancestry. In form they are peculiar to Sardinia, and were probably locally made; in fact the marble ones from Senorbì and Porto Ferro have been analysed and shown to have been made of Orani marble, and the calcite of one from Conca Illonis is also native. Like the bull's-head decoration on some of the tombs (Sedini, Sennori, Calancoi, Anghelu Ruju and Castelsardo dell'Elefante), the distribution of these idols shows a marked concentration in the north-west of the island and in the Oristano district. Almost all the smaller examples have been associated with rock-cut tombs or with Monte D'Accoddi. Several larger ones are also reported from open sites. One from Senorbì in the south (44 cm. high) had evidently stood upright in a stone setting, and must have had a public cult significance. Ozieri ware was found in the vicinity. Others said to be similar were found at Simaxis not far from Oristano where a Copper Age site was recently intersected by a canal, at Conca Illonis (Cabras) and at Puisteris. The statuettes usually have a rounded head, flat like the rest of the body, with only the nose indicated, and very rarely, the eyes. A V-shaped incision at the neck is sometimes present, and the breasts may be shown. The arms occupy a horizontal position in front of the body, from which they may be separated by a space. Unlike the Cycladic examples, the legs are not represented, and the stump-like terminal to the body has been compared with some statue-idols from Haghia Triada and Kumasa. Cretan analogies can also be found for the small marble idols from Anghelu Ruju tombs XII and XXIII. The Portoferro statuette had

Plates 5, 6

Plate 5

45

at sometime been broken across the neck and carefully repaired.

These Ozieri people may have had limited access to copper, but metal played a very minimal part in their economy, and has rarely been reported.

We now pass on to some of the main sites where this culture has been identified.

The cave of San Michele is by no means the only one to have been frequented by these people, though it may have had a magico-religious significance unlike the other caves. Of major importance because of its stratigraphy, is the cave of San Bartolomeo near Cagliari. The excavations, first reported in 1898, were unfortunately carried out at a time when exact observation of the stratigraphy was not regarded as necessary, and we have conflicting accounts of the finds. The lower levels may have belonged to a habitation site which, according to the recent reinterpretation of the finds by Atzeni, produced Ozieri ware. Above this, and perhaps associated with a group of burials, both Beaker and Bonnanaro ware were found together, and above this again was Monte Claro ware (see p. 72). Two copper daggers, a flat copper axe, perforated shell beads, a polished stone axe and many other stone and obsidian implements were also recovered, but their relationship with the various levels is uncertain. Other sites on Capo

Plate 22

Sant'Elia, such as Bagno Penale have also produced finds which show that the headland, perhaps an island at that time, supported quite a large population.

In the north of the island a cave was explored at Monte Maiore near Thiesi. Here Ozieri pottery was found with finely made arrowheads, stratified above a level with rough and mostly undecorated pottery, obsidian and flint imple-ments, but no arrowheads.

Again in the north, this time in the Gallura, Ozieri pottery has been recovered from the cave of Monte Incappiddatu near Arzachena.

Further south, at Macomer, a rock-shelter known as S'Adde was excavated some years ago, but again, unfortunately, scientific criteria were neglected. The prehistoric stratum was 1.60 metres deep and produced much burnt material and food waste. The pottery consisted of a tripod and a jar with tunnel handles of Ozieri type. The stone industry of basalt, flint, obsidian and lava, all of which are local, sometimes shows minute pressure flaking, again characteristic of a Copper Age date, and included axes, and barbed, leaf-shaped arrowheads. Some flint flakes resembling microliths could be either earlier or contemporary. The most interesting discoveries, however, were two stone figurines and two other pieces believed to be such, all roughly made of basalt, except one, the so-called 'Venus'. The interest of the first two lies in the naturalistic style in which they are portrayed; it is, in fact, immediately apparent that they have nothing at all in common with the stylised idols we have already described. The best-preserved figurine from Macomer recalls some of the Upper Palaeolithic examples from the Landes and the Dordogne, and Lilliu has suggested that we may be dealing with a lingering survival of that tradition brought to Sardinia from France, Spain or even Africa. He suggests that any cult which these Sardinian figures represented was evidently quickly swamped by the new and stronger impact of eastern Mediterranean cults. An alternative view would be that it is precisely to these East Mediterranean cults that our Venus should be attributed. That tenuous links with the Upper Palaeolithic artistic style persisted into the third or second millennium or so, is, perhaps, a less convincing hypothesis than that which treats the Venus as one of the many such figures spread widely over the East Mediterranean in the Neolithic and the Copper Age, and in rare examples represented in the Italian peninsula as well, as for instance at Savignano, near Modena. As we have already suggested when discussing the burials from Li Muri, Arzach-

Plates 7-9

ena, it is feasible that sporadic landings in Sardinia of Eastern peoples may date from the third millennium; but in view of the other finds from the cave at Macomer, it is not impossible that the whole of the deposit belongs to the period of the Ozieri pottery.

The Venus, with one other roughout, was evidently found in a hole between the rock and a stone leant against it: the hole was filled with earth and small stones. Basalt arrowheads were said to have come from the same place. Of the other figures, one, perhaps male, was found at a depth of half a metre under the present level.

Village sites have also produced evidence of the Ozieri culture, notably those of San Gemiliano, Sestu, and Conca Illonis near Oristano. The San Gemiliano village is spread out over a terraced slope. It has never been excavated, but was found when a road cutting revealed the hut foundations in section. A great deal of material has been collected, including obsidian and stone implements, Ozieri and Beaker-inspired pottery, and one fragment skilfully decorated with wide parallel white-filled grooves separated by a red slipped band. The general affinities lie with San Bartolomeo and Anghelu Ruju as well as San Michele. The hut floors measured about 4–5 metres in diameter, and appear to have been filled with ash, shells, obsidian flakes and pottery without any stratification. It is to be hoped that excavations will be carried out here before very long, so that the plans of the huts can be revealed. This can be regarded as the type-site for domestic Ozieri ware, and offers a far greater variety than the cave of San Michele or other burial places.

Plate 10

Fig. 16

ROCK-CUT
TOMBS

The rock-cut tombs appear to be the characteristic monument of these peoples, and over 1,000, varying greatly in plan and design, survive in the island, and more are being discovered at frequent intervals. They may be found singly, in small groups or forming larger cemeteries, and they may be either cut down into the ground or quarried into the rock face, and approached by a short pit-entrance or long rock-cut 'dromos'.

The most famous of the cemeteries is at Anghelu Ruju, a few miles from Alghero. Here over 35 tombs have so far been identified and excavated. They were all cut down into the ground, and were accidentally discovered during quarrying for sandstone; probably others, as yet unknown, will come to light in the course of time. In plan the tombs naturally vary, but not infrequently a large burial chamber with smaller chambers radiating from it is reached by a long passage sloping down from the entrance steps; the passage too may have chambers leading off it. Others are much simpler. The chambers themselves may be oval or rectangular in plan, and have rounded or flat ceilings, but no chronological significance seems to underlie the choice. The squared doorways giving access to the chambers, and originally closed with slabs, are sometimes carved like the lintel of a wooden door; they may be decorated above or at the sides with carved bulls' heads in relief, a feature sometimes found in other rock-cut tombs though apparently confined to the north-west corner of the island. In two instances sandstone pillars were left standing as additional supports to the roof, or as decorative features, and these, too, were sometimes carved with bulls' heads, or what are rather unconvincingly claimed to be high-prowed ships but which may in fact be simply stylised versions of the same motif. Sometimes the bulls' heads were painted with red ochre.

The finds from these tombs are the richest in Sardinia, and among the richest of the period in the west of Europe. They have recently been made the subject of a study by Audibert who for the first time distinguished the two elements underlying the pottery styles, small objects and religious concepts; his conclusions have since been newly evaluated and modified by Bray. As we now know, the two main elements which

Plate 11

Fig. 6

Fig. 6. Bull's-head frieze from a tomb at Anghelu Ruju. (After Contu)

combine at Anghelu Ruju and many other sites are represented by the Ozieri culture of East Mediterranean origin, and the Beaker and Chassey-Fontbouïsse element (sometimes here collectively called 'Western') of south-west French derivation. Probably belonging to the latest phase of the cemetery are a few sherds of Monte Claro ware. There is also a little poly-chrome ware, red and yellow, which certainly does not seem to have belonged either to the Ozieri or 'Western' traditions.

Collective burial was the normal rite, but there were two examples of cremation, and in one tomb a baby's skeleton was found in a jar.

The small finds included obsidian flakes and cores, flint arrowheads (some barbed and tanged), whetstones and bracers, a flat metal axe, tanged copper daggers, awls of Beaker type with squared section, a silver ring, spheroid stone mace-heads,

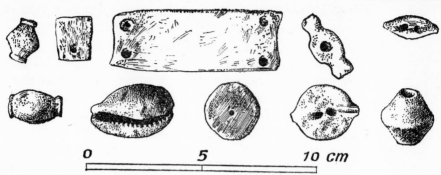

Fig. 7. 'Tortoise' and other beads, etc. from Tomb XXX at Anghelu Ruju

axe-amulets, shell pendants, perforated teeth or stones, V-bored buttons and 'tortoise' beads and marble idols of the type we have described above. Some extremely interesting results were obtained when the ores of certain copper implements from Anghelu Ruju were analysed. Three awls and a dagger were found to have been probably Spanish in origin, one dagger and one awl had a South French or Sardinian origin, one ring was East European, and a flat axe and an awl were found to have come from the British Isles, probably Ireland.

Figs. 7, 8

Plate 12

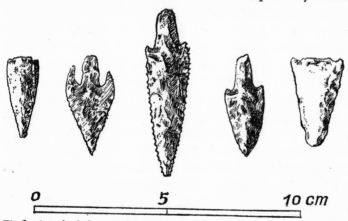

Fig. 8. Arrowheads from Anghelu Ruju

Many other individual tombs, cemeteries and funerary caves are concentrated around Alghero and Sassari. At Abbiu (Sorso) three tombs, each with several chambers, contained a number of skeletons, some of which were protected with stone settings. The grave goods are not published, but are said to have affinities with Anghelu Ruju.

Probably of the same cultural affinity were some burials in a cave at Rureo (Alghero). Here the bodies had been buried wearing necklaces of beads made of coral and human teeth, etc.

A fine tomb recently found at Santu Pedru opens off the north side of the road from Alghero to Sassari and Ittiri. A long stone-cut dromos leads into the ante-chamber from which the main chamber with squared internal pillars is reached by a short flight of steps. Other chambers lead off the main one at various levels, and in one of these two pairs of horns were carved in relief. Evidently built by people of the Ozieri culture whose grave goods included tripods and two Beakers, the tomb was later re-used by people who left large numbers of Bonnanaro type pots.

At Su Crucifissu Mannu, south of Porto Torres, seven out of a group of 19 tombs have so far been explored, and found to contain 'Cycladic' type idols, copper objects, a little decor-ated pottery and some tripods, and an axe-type handle of Bonnanaro style. The numerous chambers were entered from a narrow pit and short corridor, and in one instance some votive hollows for offerings or libations had been cut in the rock outside one of the chambers. Many skeletons were re-covered, and one of the skulls had been trepanned. With the exception of one other, thought to have been of nuragic date, this is the only trepanation so far known from Sardinia.

Close to the last-named tombs are two other groups, recently excavated by Contu, at Marinaru and Ponte Secco. At Marinaru several tombs had been cut below ground level as at Anghelu Ruju. In one of the cells of Tomb I several

Plate 14

Beakers were found with a 'Cycladic' idol and a single burial. Plate 16
Associated with them, or possibly belonging to slightly later
burials (the tomb had been too much disturbed for us to be
perfectly sure) were plain pots and some Ozieri sherds. There
is unlikely to have been a significant difference in date between
these groups. The plain wares included a hemispherical bowl, Plate 15
another with a perforated lug and omphalos base, a pot re⁄
sembling a very devolved Beaker in form, and various out⁄
turned rims. One or two of these pots belong to the Monte
Claro facies. The other finds, long flint knives, cardium shells,
mollusc beads, a long triangular obsidian arrowhead, etc.,
are all in accordance with the late Copper Age to which the
tomb belongs.

At Ponte Secco the tombs were cut into a cliff, and had
again been disturbed in Roman times. One tomb which was
excavated had several side⁄chambers leading from a large
rectangular one containing the remains of about three persons.
With them were a plano⁄convex bracer, pottery of Fontbouïsse
type and finely made barbed⁄and⁄tanged arrowheads, more
like a Pyrenean variety than any others found in Sardinia.
Other cells produced a bone 'tortoise' bead, a fragment of a
bone idol with two holes drilled for mending it at the neck,
Beaker and Ozieri ware, shell beads, boars' teeth, obsidian,
another barbed⁄and⁄tanged arrowhead, etc. Only two or three
individuals had been buried in each cell.

Further south at S. Andrea Priu, several tombs were cut
into a vertical cliff of trachite. Originally there was quite a *Fig. 9*
large group of about twenty tombs; some have been obliterated
by landslides, but three particularly interesting ones remain
and are identifiable by a deep groove cut horizontally above Plate 17, *Fig. 10*
them in the rock. All three contained skeuomorphic renderings
of architectural features: pilasters, roof⁄beams springing either
from a ledge or from the floor, and rafters, all faithfully copied
in the rock. All three tombs had been violated in antiquity,

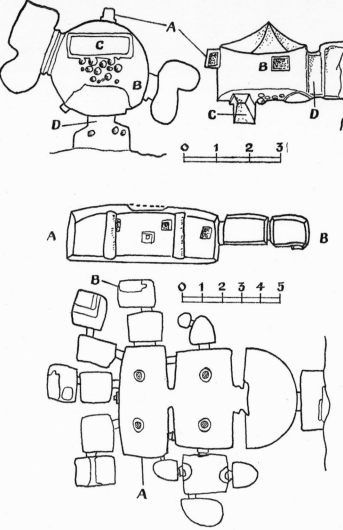

Fig. 9. Plans and sections of tombs at S. Andrea Priu (Bornorva). Scale in metres.

but others in the same group produced Copper Age pottery, a tanged triangular arrowhead, etc. At the time of their ex-cavation the sophisticated construction of these tombs led to the suspicion that they may have belonged to a much later period, and were perhaps influenced from Etruria, but in the light of the discovery of similar features at San Pedru and other rock-cut tombs, and with the recognition of comparable sophistications at an early date both in Malta and Sicily, a

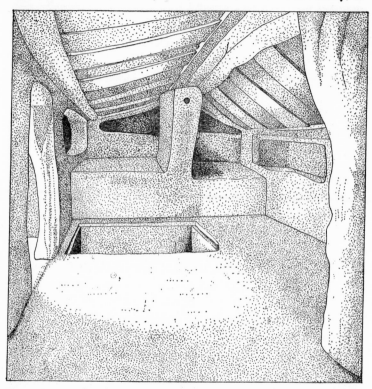

Fig. 10. Interior of tomb at S. Andrea Priu, showing imitation rafters and burial recesses

date not later than about the middle of the second millennium seems to fit the evidence.

Four others at Noeddale (Ossi) are very like the S. Andrea Priu tombs. Three of these had a single chamber, but one of them had a funerary alcove and pits for votive offerings cut in the centre of the floor. The fourth was much bigger and complex in plan, with eight chambers. The main chamber had a well-cut ridge beam running along its main axis and small rafters of rectangular section joining it. In a smaller chamber nine radiating grooves imitated the roof supports of a circular hut, and another contained a big funerary alcove with ledges and pilasters. At least one doorway seems to have been carved with an 'eared' relief moulding above, as in the case of the Sicilian tombs at Thapsos which contained Mycenaean imports, and like a tomb at Busachi and elsewhere. Further excavations carried out recently have not yet been fully published, but handles of Bonnanaro type are said to have come from the antechamber, and grooved pottery of Monte Claro type from an internal chamber. Somewhat similar architectural features are recorded from Li Coruneddi (Sassari).

At Busachi two groups of these tombs were excavated by Taramelli. One of them had a red-filled incision around the portal, the sides of which were also painted in red. Above it was a relief moulding of a horizontal line with upturned ends, the whole outlined in red, and the same colour had been used to paint a circle on the ceiling of the antechamber. The pottery seems to have affinities with Bonnanaro and with sites in the Iglesiente. Another site is at Bonnanaro itself where a tomb was cut in the limestone. From an antechamber the entrance opened into a rectangular chamber with a flat ceiling, and beyond this was a smaller rectangular chamber with a rounded ceiling and with four oval holes cut near the four corners of the chamber. There were two skeletons and a lot of plain pots of simple forms, and tripods; all of these have close affinities in particular with the cave sites in the Iglesiente. A bronze ring was also found. Although this tomb was close to Beaker sites, no vestiges of this ware were found in it, and it seems reasonable to suppose that the tomb post-dated the period of Beaker duration. The same type of pottery came from a small tomb near Cuglieri with at least five skeletons. Some other extremely interesting painted tombs have recently been reported from Mandra Antine near Thiesi. One, painted in red and black, had a design resembling Horus wings like New Kingdom tombs in Egypt.

Between Cuglieri and Oristano a very interesting single-chambered tomb was excavated at Is Araus (San Vero Milis). There were many disturbed burials with Ozieri and Beaker-derived ware as well as plain vases, evidently secondary. This suggests that the tomb was built by Ozieri people and re-used by makers of Bonnanaro pottery. The slab closing the portal was carved with two pairs of 'breasts' and a possible face. Lilliu has compared this with others from the Aegean and Corsica but the Beaker sherds lead us to seek alternative analogies from the megaliths in south-west France and Spain, and in fact the statue menhirs from Aveyron, Hérault and Gard are not dissimilar. This anthropomorphic slab is the only one of its kind in Sardinia, unless the stone closing a tomb at Chirighiddu (Abbasanta), said to have four mamil-lary protruberances, was similar.

We should also mention a few interesting tombs from the south of the island. A very recent excavation of two *domus* tombs at San Benedetto in the Iglesiente has proved them to belong to Ozieri people of San Gemiliano affinities. The finds are said to consist of fine flint knives, long leaf-shaped tanged arrowheads and pottery, as well as at least 30 skeletons which are now being studied; the skulls are said at first glance to be exclusively dolicocephalic or mesocephalic, and (unlike at Anghelu Ruju) not to include any brachycephalic ones which might suggest Beaker admixture.

Recent field work near Cagliari by Atzeni has revealed a most interesting tomb at Pimentel; it is simple in plan with a pit entrance leading into a small antechamber giving access to the small main chamber at a lower level. The rock above the

Plate 18

entrance was decorated above with carved symbols emphasised in red, which are clearly of East Mediterranean origin. These are double-looped spirals (like the eye of a hook-and-eye) and long boat-shaped signs with an inturned spiral at each end, the latter almost degenerating into the so-called 'boat' symbol at Anghelu Ruju, etc. Frankfort suggested that both these signs had a fertility significance and could be related to the ancient symbol for the goddess Ninharsag. Both forms present on the Pimentel tomb are widespread in the East Mediterranean, and several copper objects with the same motif are found even in Danubian II cultures. The loop-shaped form appears at Mycenae together with a bull which represents the male element. On the other hand at Castelluccio (Sicily) it is the looped sign which represents the male element: evidently a confusion of its sexual representation had taken place, and only its fertility character remembered. These symbols were well known in Mesopotamia as early as the Early Dynastic period and are found all over Asia from Lothal in the east to Troy and Poliochni in the west. Examples are known from the Gargano peninsula, and the Picene cemeteries, and in Phoenician contexts they last from about the fourteenth to the seventh century B C or later. No dating evidence can therefore be claimed for the Pimentel tomb, but its eastern Mediterranean inspiration cannot be denied.

Graffiti or scratched designs are reported from one tomb at Mores and are said to be similar to others from the Grotta Verde, Alghero. In neither case, however, can we be sure that they were not the work of subsequent intruders.

From the evidence we have presented, we can claim with some certainty that the rock-cut tombs were introduced by Ozieri people, and continued to be used by their descendants and other groups after their own culture had waned. We shall later argue that the dolmens were introduced into Sardinia a little before the middle of the second millennium, and that these evolved into the Giants' Graves of the Nuragic period. During this transition, and even later, rock tombs continued to be made probably even well on into the Nuragic period.

We must now describe the last major site built by people of the Ozieri culture: the remarkable sacred monument of Monte D'Accoddi.

The so-called 'altar' or 'high place' of Monte d'Accoddi is one of the most puzzling and interesting monuments in Sardinia, and its true character is not yet understood. It stands a few hundred yards to the west of the Porto Torres road, 11 km. from Sassari, on an almost imperceptible rise in the flat land which is bounded to the west by the mountains of the Nurra. A short distance away are the rock-cut tombs of Su Cruci-fissu, Marinaru and Ponte Secco.

MONTE D'ACCODDI

What at first sight seems like a large tumulus, is found, on closer examination, to be an artificial mound of earth and stones, revetted with huge blocks of limestone set in rough courses, each slightly inset over the one below. The result is a truncated pyramid rising from an irregular foundation about 30 metres square. The walls still stand to a height of about 6 metres, and may originally have reached as much as ten. On the south a trapeze-shaped ramp slopes up to the 'podium'.

Plate 19

Excavations were begun here in 1952, but unfortunately, though several seasons' work have been carried out, no very clear picture of the stratigraphy is available, and no sections have been published. A test excavation on the north side of the monument shows that about 2 metres of soil have accumulated against the foundation courses. This may possibly conceal an entrance which, if found, would help to explain the significance of the site. In the meantime it is regarded with some reserve as an altar or 'high place' of ultimately East Mediterranean inspiration, and quite unique in European prehistory.

Plate 20

The evidence of occupation around is complicated and no

doubt it covered several centuries. Its initial date, to judge from pottery and objects found both inside and under the monument, seems to have been at the turn of the Copper and Early Bronze Age, and Contu has postulated a provisional date in the fifteenth, with later occupation in the fourteenth century B C. The finds include huge numbers of tanged arrowheads of flint and obsidian, green stone axes (one decorated with incisions) and others in black stone, numbers of 'Cycladic' idols of various forms, many spindle whorls, loom weights (some pyramidal), bone objects, a copper pend-ant, bronze awls and large quantities of pottery. This is said to include tripods, carinated pots with high, perforated legs, a small square-based perforated pot, Beaker ware and pottery characteristic of San Michele (Ozieri), Anghelu Ruju and Villa Claro. There are some big pots with triple 'tunnel' handles of Maltese type (from levels pre-dating the building of the ramp). The decoration takes the form of concentric semicircles of oblique punctations made before firing, hyphen-ated bands or triangles, and triangles filled with dots and commas, zigzags, concentric circles, simple or double spirals, etc. Handles may be of the strip or ring varieties, and there are long horizontal or vertical perforated lugs. Suspension holes are very common. Bonnanaro pottery seems to date from after the monument's collapse.

Remains of later occupation near by have revealed a big rectangular hut destroyed by fire in the Early Bronze Age. From this hut came a small idol of Anatolian or Balkan type, elliptical in shape, with lateral concavities. The animal bones include ox, sheep, pig and boar, and there are also many sea shells.

Various carefully shaped stones and several standing stones are to be found in the vicinity, and a large area around the monument will need to be stripped before its full complexity can be understood. This is a site which is unique in Italian, or indeed European prehistory, and its full excavation and publication with detailed plans and sections is awaited with the greatest interest.

But even with so little knowledge at our disposal, one significant fact stands out. The technical ability to construct a building of this nature with huge blocks of stone is soon to be met again in the nuraghi. Whoever was responsible for build⁄ing Monte d'Accoddi could equally well have built the earliest nuraghi as far as technical skill is concerned. It is no longer necessary to postulate the arrival of yet another wave of immi⁄grants bringing with them new constructional techniques from the East Mediterranean, for these had already arrived. A relatively simple translation of the round hut with stone walls and conical timber roof (as shown in a skeuomorph in the rock⁄cut tombs of S. Andrea Priu, etc.) into the simplest form of nuragic tower built with overlapping courses to decrease the diameter (just as at Monte d'Accoddi) is now no longer difficult to visualise.

Plate 17

As we have seen from the tombs at Anghelu Ruju and elsewhere, it is a common occurrence to find Chassey⁄Font⁄bouïsse and Beaker pottery alongside that of Ozieri type. Most of the Chassey⁄Fontbouïsse ware comes from Anghelu Ruju, and most of it comprises plain pots with vertically pierced bosses, and sometimes with omphalos bases. There are also channelled pots belonging to types which were contemporary with Beakers in south⁄west France, and which found their way as far afield as Malta (Ġgantija and Tarxien phases). The same origin is possible for the vases decorated with incised triangles filled with pointillé decoration, like a little pot from Mannias; but the design is widespread and might have its ancestry in Spain, Italy, or further afield. Eleven of the Anghelu Ruju tombs produced this 'Western' ware, and Audibert suggested that the double perforation of some of the lugs, and the channelled ware itself, imply a Copper Age date con⁄

CHASSEY⁄
FONTBOUÏSSE
WARES

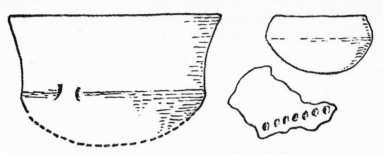

Fig. 11. Sketch of pottery from Santo Stefano, Villamarina. About 1 :4

temporary with the Beakers in south-west France. He pointed out that it is along the south French coast that carinated pots, channelled ware, omphalos bases and many of the small objects find their analogies, and Arnal had already demon-strated that 'tortoise' beads are found only in the same part of France or in Portugal. Bray has emphasised in his thesis that these pottery forms and small objects do not occur together in any one culture either in France, or in Italy where some features can be paralleled from Gaudo, Remedello, etc. Most of them therefore probably arrived as trade exchanges rather than with actual settlers, though these may have come into Sardinia in small numbers: for instance the finds from S. Stefano in Maddalena may have belonged to just one or two boat-loads of immigrants.

Fig. 11

Here in a small rock-shelter in the granite an occupation level about 40 cm. thick contained food remains, worked obsidian and quartz, a microlithic 'crescent' and other flakes with retouched edges, as well as pottery showing rounded bases and out-turned rims and two reconstructible forms: one bowl had a diameter of about 20.5 cm., outcurved rim above a vertical, rather concave neck rising from a carination and rounded base. A smaller, hemispherical pot had a slight shoulder angle, and a third fragment was decorated with a row of oval impressions. All this pottery, like the 'Western' ware from other sites, looks to south-west France for its ancestry, but this is the first time it has been found unassociated with other wares in Sardinia.

Plain pottery of uncertain affinities underlay Ozieri ware in a sealed stratum at Monte Maiore, and as we have already seen, another variety of plain pottery, which is as yet unfortunately not identified, was found at Li Muri, Arzachena and from other sites in the Gallura.

Also pointing to a limited number of settlers is the skeletal evidence from Anghelu Ruju, where ten brachycephalic (Beaker?) skulls were found with 53 dolicocephalic ones, but one must remember that the earliest settlers in Sardinia may themselves have been of mixed stock. On the whole, however, the almost invariable association of Eastern and Western elements supports the hypothesis that the Western ones were largely imported and maybe regarded as luxuries more suited for accompanying the dead than for enhancing the material equipment of the living.

The Sardinian Beakers have all come from burials, either in caves (e.g. San Bartolomeo) or from rock-cut tombs not far from the coast, and in one instance (Nuraxinieddu near Oristano) from a rectangular grave lined with stone slabs. Here an extended inhumation was the only burial, and with it were at least two Beakers and a tripod pot.

So far at least 13 Beakers are represented in Sardinia, and about the same number of tripod bowls of Ozieri form but decorated in a purely Beaker style. A fine example came from Marinaru; another, with omphalos base and decoration on the lower part, from San Bartolomeo, has the unusual feature of a little handle.

At Cuguttu a rock-cut tomb was revealed by stone-workers just outside Alghero, but partly destroyed before Taramelli was able to observe it. Bones, pottery and other finds were scattered in the various chambers, and the assemblage cannot be regarded

THE BEAKER
ELEMENT

Plate 21

Plates 15, 16

Plate 24

with certainty as a closed group, though it may be so. A handled Beaker, several pots of Bonnanaro type, a quadrangular sectioned awl, two thin copper bracelets, a flat metal spiral bead, a steatite axe-amulet, beads, pendants, obsidian and flint knives were recorded, as well as big mace-heads, perhaps used for cutting the tomb.

At San Bartolomeo, Beakers and Bonnanaro ware seem to have been found in the same level overlying Ozieri ware and below Monte Claro pots. At Marinaru and San Pedru the Beakers were primary in rock-cut tombs.

Polished black Beaker sherds of Pyrenean affinities came from a rock-cut tomb at Sas Lacheddos, and at Marinaru and elsewhere the Beakers are decorated with bands of alternate left and right oblique hyphenated lines between plain bands: a motif which, like the plain lozenges on hatched bands from Anghelu Ruju, is also common in the Pyrenees and south-west France.

Metal objects associated with these imports are rare, but a few tanged copper daggers are recorded from San Bartolomeo and Anghelu Ruju, and from the Grotta Sant'Elia, near Cagliari, came a rivetted dagger with rounded butt and slight midrib. Very few copper axes of this date are known. One from San Bartolomeo has a splayed blade, and a slightly flanged one was found at Anghelu Ruju. It is said that a 'spearhead' was found at Su Crucifissu Mannu. Spiral copper-wire beads from Cuguttu and Anghelu Ruju have analogies in some French caves and in some objects found at sites in Sicily such as Monteracello, Matrensa and Melilli.

By far the commonest metal implement is the awl with squared section. These were found at Cuguttu, Anghelu Ruju, San Bartolomeo and other sites, and one from Sant'Elia was still mounted in its bone handle.

These metal objects are all perfectly at home in a Beaker context and may have come into Sardinia with the other Western imports.

Rounded V-bored buttons came from Anghelu Ruju, and we have already spoken of the 'tortoise' beads with their analogies from Aude, as well as from Portugal which is less likely to have been their immediate origin, as their accompanying objects are absent there.

Finally, we should remember the stone bracers which are occasionally reported in Sardinia and which are a classic Beaker accompaniment. Several examples were discovered at Anghelu Ruju and a plano-convex one from Ponte Secco. Another came from the ossuary of Settimo San Pietro, Cagliari.

There is no evidence for a pure Beaker culture in Sardinia, and the Beakers, together with the Chassey-Fontbouïsse pottery and many small objects presumably reached the island as imports from south France. Other trade contacts probably existed with Corsica, the Italian mainland and Iberia; with the last two regions the exchanges increased gradually to culminate in the later first millennium.

There seems little reason to doubt that the Ozieri people introduced the rock-cut tombs into Sardinia, for they are tombs which are alien to the Beaker or Chassey-Fontbouïsse people who represent the other major element discernible in the earliest prehistoric cultures of Sardinia, and who appear to be contemporary with them. We have therefore to search for prototypes of these tombs which antedate the Beakers and other Western elements belonging to the early second millennium.

ORIENTAL ORIGINS

There are no very comparable tombs from the West Mediterranean. In mainland Italy (e.g., Rinaldone, Gaudo, etc.) there are numerous *tombe a forno*, but they are unlikely to be earlier than the Sardinian ones. The Gaudo tombs are collective, and might be related: an approximately contemporary date is provided by a copper midrib dagger.

From Malta the tombs at Xemxija are collective, and some contained pottery belonging to the Mġarr phase. But these tombs continue into the later phases of Maltese prehistory when the simple type of temple was developing several sets of chambers, and culminate in the Tarxien period, just at a time in fact when Maltese influence can be discerned in the Ozieri 'tunnel' handles, and in some of the decorative motifs on the pottery. And at Hal Saflieni, sherds with Ozieri affinities came from a horizon which a V-bored button should date to the Copper Age. It is not improbable, too, that the channelled ware from the Ġgantija phase in Malta reached there from Sardinia.

Figs. 5, 6
Plates 5–9, 18

But the religious conceptions of the Ozieri people all point to the East Mediterranean: the bulls' heads, the marble idols, the incised pebble from San Michele itself, possibly the Macomer 'Venus', and certainly the Pimentel fertility designs. The possibility of an origin for the tombs in the same region cannot therefore be discounted, particularly since the curvilinear decoration of the Ozieri pottery has frequently been recognised to have affinities with, or indeed to be probably derived from, the painted wares from Crete and elsewhere from the Middle Minoan II period onwards. And the tripods and flower-pots (or pyxides) have their closest analogies in the east.

Rock-cut tombs for single burials belonging to the Early Cycladic period have been found in the Cyclades (at Syros, Euboea, etc.), and the marble idols of Cycladic type, which must certainly be related to the Sardinian ones, were being imported into Crete in Early Minoan III. The possibility of direct inspiration in the third millennium cannot therefore be dismissed. Moreover the rite of collective burial in Sardinia has its counterpart in the East Mediterranean at Zigouries, dated by Blegen to Early Helladic II and III. Chronologically, however, the eastern dates seem too early to fit the Sardinian evidence, and a less direct inspiration would seem more likely.

In Sicily the rock-cut tombs most relevant to the Sardinian ones come from Malpasso and the Conca d'Oro, but appear to belong to just the same Beaker horizon as the Sardinian ones, and Bray has suggested that the tomb type arrived in west Sicily together with Beakers from Sardinia, slightly before the Castelluccio period began (around 1800 B C, accord-ing to Bernabò Brea). The Gaudo (Paestum) tombs could have the same derivation. This date for the Beakers in Sardinia would fit the evidence extremely well. For the Chassey-Fontbouïsse pottery together with the Beakers and other objects associated with the south French Copper Age should, according to the French evidence, belong to just that chrono-logical horizon.

As we have seen, Beaker pottery has been primary in some Sardinian rock-cut tombs. This implies that the tomb type had already been introduced by the Ozieri people. At the cave of San Bartolomeo the stratification revealed Beakers later than Ozieri ware, but generally the two are found together. It is therefore improbable that the Ozieri people arrived in Sardinia much, if at all, before the dawn of the second millennium. Perhaps they were prospectors seeking a new source of obsidian when too much rivalry made that of the Lipari islands difficult of access, and when improved naviga-tion opened up the routes via the south coast of Sicily instead of through the Messina straits.

THE BONNANARO CULTURE

In the last section we saw that Beakers were stratified at San Bartolomeo in the same levels as pottery which is usually known as Bonnanaro ware (after the rock-cut tomb where it was first found). Subsequently it was discovered in a number of natural caves in the Iglesiente, thought to belong to the Bronze Age, after about 1500 B C when the Ozieri culture was dying out. In the light of recent research we now know that this culture is distributed all up the western half of Sardinia, to the west of an imaginary line from Sassari to Cagliari, but more field work in the eastern half of the island may radically alter the distribution pattern. It is not improbable, too, that we may have to date the first appearance of this pottery rather earlier than the mid second millennium, at least in the six-teenth century B C, but so far we cannot be sure of this. The culture is represented exclusively by pottery, and there does not seem to be any characteristic metal or stone industry.

Fig. 12

This pottery is almost always quite plain and much less well finished than the Ozieri ware, from which it is always clearly distinguishable. It is much less easy to distinguish it from the simpler nuragic forms.

Generally brownish in colour, though varied according to the firing, the shapes include simple hemispherical or cylin-drical bowls, sometimes with bosses or protruberances above the rim. Another common form is the tripod, often with straight flared sides and legs more or less rectangular in section:

Plate 25

some of these tripods are carinated and some have simple ring handles. Elbow handles with upturned point, long, jutting ledge handles, or rounded, almost solid ones, pierced with only a tiny hole, also occur, as well as double or triple-lobed lugs. The repertoire includes handled platters, biconical pots, and a lot of very diminutive forms. At Fanne Massa near Cuglieri, a small rock-cut tomb which had been disturbed contained remains of five people with a quantity of these pots, and among them was a bowl divided inside into four sections. Comparable examples came from Barumini in an eighth–seventh century B C context, and from other Nuragic period sites at Serra Orrios and elsewhere; and although the form may have originated at the time of the Bonnanaro culture, we may have to recognise the Fanne Massa pot as a later insertion into the tomb.

It is in the Iglesiente that this ware is found in greatest abundance, associated with inhumation burials in the natural caves which are particularly common in that part of the island.

Fig. 12. Forms of Bonnanaro ware. (Not to scale)

At S'Orreri near Fluminimaggiore, a hollow had been scooped in the cave floor to contain the burial, around which a number of bowls, handled bowls and other simple-shaped pots were placed. Perhaps worn on the body at the time of burial were the hollow ribbed bone pin (perhaps a hairpin) and a baked clay ring, the size of a pendant. In a second 'chamber' were found an obsidian core, leaf-shaped arrow-heads, and a piece of polished dolerite axe. In a third recess which was like a cleft in the rock, the excavator found a group of carefully collected human bones and skulls, and the skull of a dog. The pottery was all roughly made except for the tripods which might have been turned on a simple wheel.

Fig. 13

69

Fig. 13. Grooved bone pin-head from S'Orreri 1:1

Fig. 13

Quite a number of other natural caves have been found to contain burials with this type of pottery: at Serbariu near Narcao, Punta Niedda near Cagliari, Villa-massargia, and Genna Luas, to mention only some of them. Sometimes, as at Su Moiu in the Sulcis, as many as 50 pots seem to have been put with the burials, which are invariably inhumations.

In one instance this pottery has been found in an oval grave flanked with upright stones; this was at Cuccuru Nuraxi (Settimo San Pietro, near Cagliari). Although only about 2 metres long, and less in width, this cist contained the remains of about 10 or 15 people: it must have been an ossuary in fact. The few pots were of Bonnanaro type, and there were bone and shell beads, fragments of metal and a copper awl and brown stone bracer. Both these last types are more commonly found in Beaker contexts. The cist had probably been covered with a big block of stone that was found beside it.

The San Bartolomeo evidence suggests that Bonnanaro pottery was introduced, or evolved locally, at a time when Beakers were still current, and this evidence is supported not only at Settimo San Pietro, but also at the rock-cut tomb at Cuguttu; though, as we have said above, this may not have been a closed group. At S'Orreri we have already drawn attention to a large, hollow, ribbed bone pin-head, found with pottery exclusively of this type. These bone pins are found in the Portuguese caves, as well as in the Early Chalcolithic of Almeria, and related types come from the south of France and elsewhere; all these seem to fall within the first half of the second millennium.

At the rock-cut tomb of Santu Pedru, Bonnanaro ware was stratified above Beakers, and at Serra Is Araus it was secondary to Ozieri ware. The evidence for its initial date is therefore likely to be around the sixteenth century BC, if we are right in thinking that little, if any, Beaker influence was apparent after about 1500 BC.

Unfortunately we cannot yet be sure whether it was brought in with settlers, or whether it evolved from the repertory which had existed for several centuries in the island. It is interesting to note that Bonnanaro pottery has been found in some Giants' Tombs, and as these almost certainly evolved from dolmens (which we shall argue in a subsequent chapter came into Sardinia in about the mid second millennium, but which have not yet yielded primary grave goods) there is just the possibility that the two arrived together. Both seem to have marked the end of the Ozieri culture. Unfortunately the pottery forms are too simple to be equated with any one specific outside culture. Many of the shapes recur in the Bronze Age wares of Apulia (from which region the dolmens reached Malta and possibly Sardinia) and many other regions as well, and not all of them find easily identified ancestry among the pre-existing Sardinian forms. It is interesting to note that one or two tripods comparable to the Bonnanaro ones were found at Leporano and Scogli del Tonno, and are now to be seen in the Taranto museum.

Whatever may have been its origin, this pottery lasted long enough to appear in some of the Giants' Tombs, but had probably died out by the time of the complex nuraghi of the Full Nuragic period. Its *floruit* may have been the second half of the second millennium, and it strongly influenced the simple Nuragic pottery forms such as those from Peppe Gallu, a site which is unlikely to ante-date the Punic period by many years.

The trade contacts already established with Sicily were evidently still continuing when Bonnanaro ware was in use, for several pots which may have been imported from Sardinia were found near Trapani.

THE MONTE CLARO CULTURE

Another culture which has only been recognised in recent years, is known by the name Monte Claro from a rock-cut tomb found near Cagliari in 1904. This was an oven-shaped tomb with a pit entrance, and it contained one or more skele-tons accompanied by a variety of pottery unidentified at the time, but about which we now know a good deal more. What we still do not know for certain is its chronological range; nor do we know whether it was brought into Sardinia from outside, or was an indigenous development, though the latter seems more probable.

Figs. 14, 15

The pottery which distinguishes this culture is very unlike both the earlier wares we have so far described (the Ozieri ware and its importations, and the Bonnanaro ware), and it is also unlike the later, Nuragic pottery. At first impression it seems to make a sudden appearance, already equipped with its repertory of distinctive shapes and ornament. There are, however, on closer aquaintance, various features which may have derived from earlier traditions.

It is much better made than the Bonnanaro series and its forms are more distinctive. The larger pots are usually brownish red or brown, and the paste may be backed with pounded quartz or obsidian. Some of the smaller and finer pots are made of a yellowish, smoother paste, and painted with red ochre before being pattern burnished with a spatula. Most of the surfaces are polished, and may be given a reddish or black slip, quite often pattern burnished with angular or rectilinear

Plate 23

(never curvilinear) designs of parallel lines, zig-zags or latticing. Most of the rest of the decoration takes the form of wide fluting made with the finger, and usually arranged in panels at right angles, stabs made with a pointed stick, or finger-nail im-pressions, sometimes filled with red and reminiscent of Ozieri ware. The repertory is lacking in imagination, and the com-

Fig. 14. Monte Claro ware forms. (Not to scale)

monest element is a herring-bone design, incised or pattern burnished.

Some of the larger jars reach a considerable size, and may be over 60 cm. tall. Generally cylindrical or curved biconical in

Fig. 15. Monte Claro ware forms. (Not to scale)

shape, they have strongly out-turned or very wide ledge rims often with impressed decoration or fluting along the upper surface. These jars may be provided with two sets of handles, one above the other. There are also big straight-sided platters, again with fluted ledge rims, and other rims are hammer-shaped like those of Roman mortaria. Some straight-necked jars have a series of perforations below the rim, and string-holes for suspension are not uncommon.

Another very characteristic form is the tripod with wide, flat or triangular legs, often decorated, attached to the junction of the walls and base with an angular shoulder. The legs are vertical, and not splayed like the Bonnanaro ones. There are several other shapes: jars, platters and dishes, occasionally with a slightly curved base, but almost invariably the base is flat.

Made of the finer, yellowish clay (again perhaps of Ozieri tradition) are carinated cups, flasks with cylindrical necks and splayed rim pots of various forms. Being of more easily break-able clay, we do not yet know the full range of shapes. The Ozieri 'tunnel' handle still sometimes persists. Occasionally, too, reserved slip decoration is used, as in the earlier tradition.

There is no characteristic industry associated with this pottery. Earlier varieties of stone, flint and obsidian implements remain unchanged, as do maces, grain-rubbers, etc. Also a little metal may have been worked, as a lava crucible was found at Enna Pruna (Mogoro) and a tanged copper blade in the Sa Duchessa tomb.

So far, this Monte Claro pottery has mostly been recorded from the Campidano, though it occurs more sporadically in the Sassari region (where it was represented both at Anghelu Ruju and at Marinaru), as well as in the Iglesiente. Coming from a post-Beaker and post-Bonnanaro level at the cave of San Bartolomeo, it is best known from village sites such as San Gemiliano (Sestu), Monte Olladiri near Monastir, and Enna Pruna near Mogoro, to mention just a few, for there are others in the Campidano, particularly in the Oristano district. It is also reported from the vicinity of what appear to be archaic nuraghi and from rock-cut tombs and cist graves as well as in

Fig. 16

natural caves. Some of these will be described below, but first let us say a little more about the villages. San Gemiliano is already well known as the type site for domestic Ozieri ware. Between 50 and 60 huts have produced Ozieri pottery, either picked up on the surface, or found in the huts sectioned by the road cutting. Another six or seven have produced Monte Claro ware as well. It is interesting to note that some nuragic period huts are grouped together at the northern edge of this village, signifying that they were either contemporary with the later occupation of the village, or that they were built afterwards in places where no earlier hut floors could be seen. With the light soil on which the village stood, the hut founda/ tions would fill up not very long after their abandonment: it can be argued, therefore, that the nuragic huts represent a continuity, both in area and in time, of the settlement's duration.

Monte Olladiri is only a few kilometres to the north of San Gemiliano, and this time the whole village belongs to the Monte Claro culture, with a sprinkling of Nuragic period huts which from their distribution seem to be broadly contempor/ ary. One or two of the Monte Claro huts evidently overlap with a lingering Ozieri tradition. Either of these villages, which together probably span a period from about the fifteenth to the thirteenth century or a little later, would provide an admirable opportunity to excavate selected huts of the three traditions represented, to see how, if at all, the plans and con/ struction varied.

There are numerous other villages of this general period in the Simaxis neighbourhood and elsewhere near Oristano; the whole of the Campidano indeed must have been thickly populated.

Another interesting village was discovered at Enna Pruna near Mogoro, and in this instance a nuraghe stood on the edge of the inhabited area. The relationship between the huts with Monte Claro pottery, including some with dotted red/

Fig. 16. Ozieri ware forms. (Not to scale)

filled decoration in the Ozieri tradition, and the various phases of the nuraghe's development cannot be worked out without excavation; but the site is promising, particularly as the elliptical chamber of the earliest phase of the nuraghe is thought to be an archaic feature.

But this is not the only site which hints at the association of Monte Claro pottery with the earliest nuraghi. There are others at Su Guventu near Mogoro, and at Is Cresieddas. The latter is in flat, stubble-covered land near Nuraminis. Monte Claro pottery can be picked up on the surface, and the very vestigial remains of a simple nuraghe can be seen within the area of the settlement. A short distance away to the east, at Is Ruinalis de Segavenu, a village of the same date has been identified on rising land, and again the remains of a nuraghe seem to be associated. At one point recent agricultural work caused a big block of stone to be pulled out of the ground, leaving a hole about 1 metre across, from which came not only Monte Claro ware, but also some undecorated pottery including a 'tunnel' handle and other fragments in an earlier tradition.

Of even greater interest is a site so far only partially excavated by Atzeni at Sa Corona, Villagreca. Here was found a building which may turn out to be either a very early nuraghe, or a large hut of megalithic construction, slightly elliptical inside. Within it were found numbers of grain rubbers, pestles and mace-heads, as well as a flat rivetted dagger of copper or bronze, and many fragments of daub retaining the imprint of wattles, either from the fallen roof, or less probably from ovens. The pottery includes some undecorated pieces with affinities in the Ozieri and Bonnanaro traditions, as well as Monte Claro ware and pottery of early Nuragic type similar to some from a Nuragic complex a few hundred metres away. Whether this is in fact an archaic nuraghe, or a building which should be regarded as ancestral to the nuraghi, it is obviously of the greatest importance, and its publication will be awaited with eager interest.

The rock-cut tomb of Villa Claro is the only rock-cut Plate 23 tomb we know which has exclusive Monte Claro pottery. Other types of tomb were also used and we have examples of cist graves from Sa Duchessa and San Gemiliano. The slab-lined grave of Ena'e Muros (Ossi), described on page 101, may also belong to this culture.

The grave at Sa Duchessa was found in 1956 only 500 metres or so from the Villa Claro tomb. It was one of at least six graves which were found accidentally and not very carefully observed. They seem to have been cut in the clayish soil and then, in one grave at least, lined with a revetment of rough stones. The burials were inhumed, and five or six pots, all characteristic of the Monte Claro culture, were placed around the heads of the skeletons. A few *mytilus* and *pectunculus* beads, stone implements and a tanged copper blade 9.1cm. long were also recovered.

At San Gemiliano a cist grave was found at the southern limit of the settlement, cut through in section by the road. As far as can be ascertained the grave was a little under 1 metre in depth and was probably rectangular. One slab of the revetment was in position and others had fallen in, and some stones seen out of place near by may have been the covering slabs. Three crouched, strongly contracted skeletons were lying in different directions on their left sides, and belonged to two adults and a child aged eight or nine. Remains of what seem to have been a bracelet and necklace made of shell beads lay near the child's head. Parts of a very large fluted jar, a plain handled mug and a platter with slightly rounded sides and rim with a relief decoration around it, accompanied the burials.

So far no very comparable pottery to the Monte Claro ware has been recognised outside Sardinia, and there is therefore good reason to suspect that it developed locally from the earlier traditions we have already described. The fluted decoration could have derived from the Chassey-Fontbouïsse grooved ware, and as we have seen, the 'tunnel' handle and tripod form both still persist. But the exclusive presence of this pottery in some sites shows that it represents a distinct and separate entity. For the moment then, and until we know more, we suggest that the Monte Claro ware developed at the end of the Ozieri tradition, i.e. about the fifteenth–fourteenth centuries, B C, and lasted sufficiently long to overlap the beginnings of the Nuragic culture. Although we have no stratigraphical proof, there is strong circumstantial evidence that some early nuraghi were associated with this pottery. At Enna Pruna and Su Guventu, Lilliu has tentatively dated the nuraghi to 1200–1000 B C, stressing that they are not typologically the most archaic form of nuraghe. On the other hand the Sa Corona megalithic hut or archaic nuraghe should be earlier than either of those sites. Very approximately, therefore, we can date the Monte Claro pottery between about the fourteenth and eleventh centuries B C or a little later. It seems to have had relatively little influence on Nuragic pottery which reveals its Bonnanaro ancestry much more noticeably.

The Monte Claro culture may, in fact, have begun rather later than that of Bonnanaro, though they must have existed side by side for some centuries, and both contributed to the gradually evolving Nuragic culture; Bonnanaro ware being found in Giants' Tombs and Monte Claro ware at least suspected of being associated with early nuraghi. Both groups were evidently current for several centuries after the middle of the second millennium. Perhaps the two traditions (or maybe the rather different ethnic groups responsible for them) gradually merged and their joint inheritance may have given rise to the Nuragic culture.

CHAPTER III

Megalithic Tombs and Standing Stones

THE 'DOLMENS'

IN THE ABSENCE of datable material from the dolmens other than the 'Bronze Age' or 'Nuragic' ware found in one or two, and which may be either primary or secondary, their chronological position can only be attempted on typological grounds until an undisturbed dolmen, complete with grave goods, comes to light.

There are, today, nearly 40 dolmens in the island, and a number more are known to have been destroyed. An interesting fact emerges when their distribution is plotted on the map, for it is then seen that they have a marked concentration up the high, boulder-strewn land on each side, but particularly to the north, of the Tirso river. Such a compact distribution suggests that the time span during which these tombs were in use was relatively limited; that they were outmoded before they became more widespread. Thus Mackenzie's hypothesis that they gradually evolved into the true Giants' Tombs seems plausible, and on a number of grounds, acceptable.

Another, smaller, group of nine dolmens (or *stazzone* as they are called locally) in the Luras district of the Gallura seems to be distinct from the main group, from which they are separated by mountainous land. It should, however, be emphasised that this separation into two groups is, as yet, hypothetical; in the absence of more information it must be admitted that either group may be an extension of the other. The Gallura dolmens, which seem to be more rectangular in plan than the Tirso group, are, like the Corsican ones near Sartène in the south-west of that island, associated with numbers of standing stones, and the two areas seem to have close affinities

Fig. 17

in this, as in many other aspects of their prehistoric settlement. One of the Corsican dolmens, that at Silogna, produced pottery of Eneolithic type.

The main group does not seem to be associated with standing stones, which are, however, frequently found close to Giants' Tombs. If, then, we accept the independence of the Tirso from the Gallura group, its distribution suggests a landing of dolmen builders at the Tirso mouth, and their gradual spread up the plateaux flanking its valley. Certainly the indigenous invention of the dolmen seems improbable, and we are led to search for parallels outside Sardinia.

For the most part the dolmens in Sardinia tend to be cur-vilinear, round or oval rather than rectangular, and this *Figs. 18, 19* characteristic differentiates them from dolmens in many parts of western and southern Europe. In south France, Corsica, the Pyrenees, Catalonia and parts of the Italian mainland, the dolmens are pronouncedly rectangular and are often made with overlapping slabs of stone rather than of irregular blocks. Nor are the Sicilian dolmens such as Monteracello comparable. Several of the Sardinian examples do, however, find analogies in Malta. Both Maone (Benetutti) and Sos Monumentos (Buddusò) were found to have a hollow grave beneath the dolmen, a feature closely paralleled at Tal Hammut in Malta which produced a sherd of Tarxien cemetery type, dated by Evans to approximately 1400 BC and by Bernabò Brea to between 1700 and 1400 BC (recently Trump has postulated that

Fig. 17. Distribution of dolmens. Birori (pair), Mesu Enas (Abbasanta), S'Angrone (Abbasanta), Cannigheddu (Abbasanta), Nurarchei (Abbasanta) (group), Sos Monu- mentos, Sa Janna de sa Laccu (Buddusò) (pair), Isella (Buddusò) (pair), Doli Fichima (Buddusò), Elcomis (Buddusò) (single), Elcomis (Buddusò) (pair), Bitti (pair), Su Coveccu (Bultei), Maone (Benetutti), S'Enna sa Vacca (Olzai) (uncertain), Lugulu (Olzai), Perdalunga (Austis), Cossoine (Sindia) (group), Monte Ferru (Esterzili), Le Casacce (Arzachena), Patruali (Arzachena), Enu Cabbas (Olbia), Luras (group)

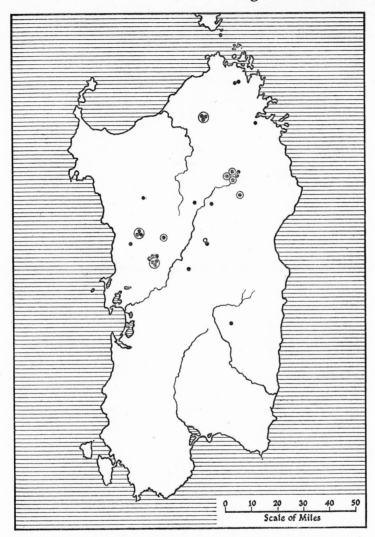

Scale of Miles

Key:

• *Single dolmen*   ◉ *Group of 3 or more*

◉ *Pair*   ○ *Unconfirmed*

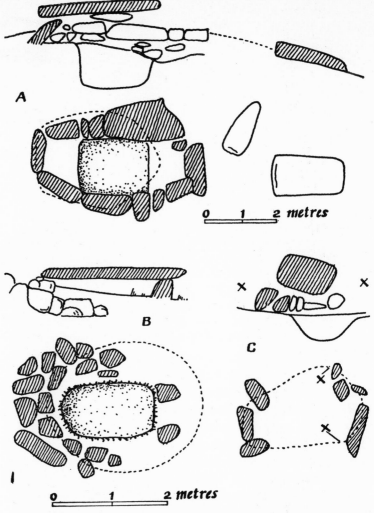

Fig. 18. Plans of dolmens with graves: (a) Maone (Benetutti), (after Mackenzie); (b) Tel Hammut (Malta), (after Evans); (c) Sos Monumentos (Buddusò); (after Taramelli)

the change from Tarxien to Tarxien Cemetery culture took place in the sixteenth century.) At least three other Maltese dolmens have the same feature. Such graves beneath dolmens are not common, though one was found with Beaker ware at

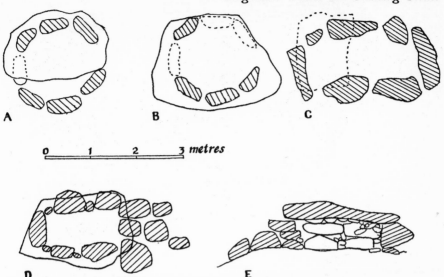

Fig. 19. Dolmens: (a) Sa Perda e S'Altare (Birori), (after Taramelli); (b) Sa Tanca sar Bogodas (Birori), (after Taramelli); (c) Cannigheddu e S'Ena (Abbasanta), (after Taramelli); (d) and (e) Doli Fichima (Buddusò); (after Mackenzie)

Collet de las Forgues (Espuñola) in Spain. If we admit the Maltese similarities, we must infer that the dolmen builders arrived in Sardinia considerably later than the rock-cut tomb builders and no long hiatus need disturb the acceptance of Mackenzie's suggestion that typologically the simple dolmen underwent a process of evolution which led to the fully devel-oped Giants' Tombs of Nuragic times.

But it would be rash to argue with conviction from such slender evidence that Sardinian dolmens were all inspired from Malta, and it should be borne in mind in this connection that both the Maltese dolmens and their analogous tombs in the Otranto district of south Italy sometimes had pierced capstones, which feature has never been recorded from Sardinia. Some intermixture of our two Sardinian groups may be suggested by such a tomb as Su Monumentu at Olzai. This

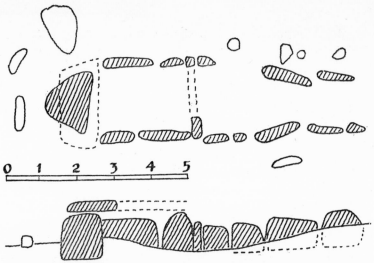

Fig. 20. *Dolmen of Perda Lunga (Austis). (After Mackenzie). Scale in metres*

was made with two long and two shorter slabs and a large capstone, and belongs more closely to the Gallura group, of which it may be an outlying example. We cannot, therefore, exclude the possibility of a spread down the Tirso valley from an immediate source in the Gallura.

As has already been said, Mackenzie's hypothesis of the gradual elongation of the simple, originally circular dolmen of Birori type into the developed Giants' Tomb is plausible. The tomb of Sos Monumentos (Buddusò), already mentioned for its Maltese affinities, had a dry stone walling lining the grave, and at one end of the dolmen there were several lines of boulders suggesting a typological development towards the Giants' Tombs. Indeed numerous tombs which may be transitional can be quoted. Doli Fichima Tomb II (Ala dei Sardi) had a rectangular cist surrounded by an apse-like stone setting recalling the Giants' Tombs, and this type may well have been followed by tombs like S'Enna sa Vacca (Olzai) and Su Coveccu (Bultei) where the same stone setting is present but a rectangular arrangement of stones replaces the

Plate 26

Fig. 18c

Figs. 19d, e

86

cist. Mackenzie claimed to have seen similar tombs, at first sight resembling much ruined Giants' Tombs, in Corsica where no actual Giants' Tombs are present.

The unique monument of Perda Lunga (Austis), which has a long rectangular corridor divided, according to Mackenzie, by a septal slab and claimed by him to be a dolmen, later elongated, and transitional between a true dolmen and a Giants' Tomb, can only be regarded as such with reserve. Giants' Tombs, as will be seen later, are never found with a divided corridor and the feature reminds one more of the gallery graves of the Bari district, or the segmented tombs of the Pyrenees and various parts of the western Mediterranean littoral.

Fig. 20

But on the whole Mackenzie's theory seems acceptable, and quite apart from typology, the fact that both dolmens and Giants' Tombs are frequently found in pairs, one presumably replacing the other when full, again supports his hypothesis. At least five pairs of dolmens have been recorded, and other groups of four or more may originally have been pairs. The same grouping in pairs or larger numbers is also recorded in Malta and in Corsica.

We have, however, to note one fact of prime importance. The dolmens were certainly intended for single, and the Giants' Tombs for collective, burial. Some radical change of fashion occurred, and the most probable explanation is that inter-mixture and cultural exchange took place between the dolmen builders and the collective burial people responsible for the

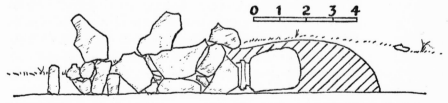

Fig. 21. Rock-cut tomb with megalithic passage at Mesu Enas (Abbasanta). (After Mackenzie). Scale in metres

87

rock-cut tombs and perhaps the tombs of Settimo San Pietro type as well, as a result of which the collective burial rite prevailed. Such an intermixture of people and rites is, indeed, reflected in some of the tomb types. At Perdas Fittas (Gavoi) a rock-cut corridor was added to a megalithic tomb, while the opposite is found both at Mesu Enas (Abbasanta) which produced sherds attributed to the Bronze Age, and not far away at S'Angrone. These stylistic influences could have begun quite early in the dolmen sequence, though in the last two instances at least, they probably belong to the period of the Giants' Tombs and the nuraghi.

To sum up then, we find dolmens with both Maltese and Corsican affinities in Sardinia; and whatever their derivation, their date is likely to fall within the Eneolithic or Bronze Age. In the case of a Corsican derivation they may have reached Sardinia around the seventeenth century B C, while if they were inspired from Malta they may have arrived a century or so later. This tomb type seems to have been fairly short-lived before fusion with people using the collective burial rite led to the evolution from the dolmen to the Giants' Tomb. A hint at a relatively late date within the period suggested is provided by the discovery of a small bowl, said to have been similar to those from near-by Giants' Tombs, in a simple dolmen rather elongated in form at Cannigheddu e S'Ena (Abbasanta). This also points to the cultural continuity between the two kinds of tomb, which has already been discussed.

In the absence of clearly primary grave goods from the Sardinian dolmens, more than this cannot be said, and the subject must be treated with reserve; so, too, must be the hypo-thesis that Bonnanaro ware may have been introduced with the dolmens. We are still too much in the dark about the origins of both the pottery and the tombs.

THE GIANTS' TOMBS

The so-called Giants' Tombs (*Tombe di Giganti*), which are widely distributed all over the islands, are characterised by a curved forecourt leading into a long, narrow, rectangular passage or chamber, made, like the wings of the forecourt, either of orthostatic slabs covered with capstones, or of coursed walling inclining inwards to form the roof. On the outside, this passage was usually rounded in plan and covered with a cairn-like structure, retained by a stone setting. The burials were placed in the passage, and the forecourt was evidently used for ritual ceremonies. In the great majority of cases the façade of these tombs faces between south and east.

Excavations of Giants' Tombs have unfortunately been extremely limited, and scientific exploration has been attempted only recently. Moreover, the pottery obtained from earlier excavations has belonged to types which had a very long life in Sardinian prehistory, and the large number of bronzes, though fairly closely datable themselves, may have been either primary or secondary in the tombs. One point does, however, emerge: the tombs undoubtedly belong to the nuraghi, and were the burial places for the family or clan inhabiting them. Often built on a slight rise, presumably for better drainage, many are to be found near nuraghi or nuragic villages in an otherwise deserted countryside, and their association need not be doubted. The two types of monument seem indeed to have developed contemporaneously.

We have already suggested that the dolmens, which prob-ably supplied one of the structural elements leading to the evolution of the Giants' Tombs, were introduced into Sardinia around the mid second millennium, at about the time of, or only a little earlier than, the supposed date of the earliest nuraghi. The evolution of the Giants' Tomb may, then, have taken place during the succeeding few centuries, and have reached full sophistication (or, alternatively, simplification) by the mid first millennium. The change-over from single to collective burial may either have been a reaction to a growing population, or, much more probably, have resulted from cul-tural exchanges between the dolmen and the rock-cut or other collective tomb builders.

Tombs of a possibly transitional type do, in fact, exist, and Mackenzie's theory seems plausible. The first to develop

Fig. 18c

may have been tombs such as Sos Monumentos (Buddusò), followed by S'Enna sa Vacca (Olzai) and others described above. These may have been followed by simple Giants' Tombs with the passage built in a megalithic construction with upright slabs covered by capstones. Later again, the passage was sometimes built with coursed masonry, and in still later and more sophisticated examples, with carefully cut wedge-shaped stones, perfectly fitting, and similar in technique to some structures inspired by contact with the Phoenicio-Punic world.

The forecourt, too, gradually grew in importance, though it seems to have been present from early examples, and may have been derived from the Maltese temples. Like the passage, the side wings of the forecourt were built with orthostatic slabs, or coursed masonry, sometimes a combination of the two, and were often provided with a seat or bench for offerings. The entrances to the tombs seem to have been made increasingly

Plate 27

monumental and were closed by a huge portal stone with an arched top indicating the height of the roof over the passage. Cut in the lower part of this slab was a small squared or rounded hole giving access to the passage or chamber.

This may present a fairly accurate picture of the general tendencies, but the sequence is purely hypothetical and based on typology only. Naturally too, it would be rash to suggest that any specific simple tomb is necessarily earlier than a more evolved type. The district in which it is found, the possibilities

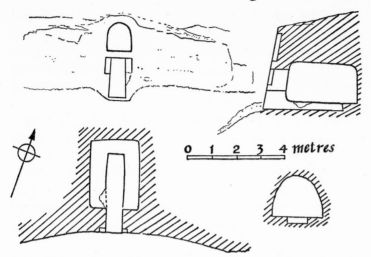

Fig. 22. Tomb at Molafà (Sassari) with façade cut in live rock in imitation of the Giants' Tombs. (After Taramelli)

of cultural contacts, the quality of the local stone, and even the ability and traditions of the builders must be borne in mind. Moreover, structural alterations to earlier tombs may have been carried out at various times.

Certainly there seems to be ample evidence for contacts between the builders of the rock⁄cut tombs and the Giants' Tombs, and interesting examples of structural 'cross⁄breeding' can be quoted. At Molafà the curved façade and tall portal stone of a typical Giants' Tomb are faithfully copied in the live rock and lead into a small rock⁄cut tomb. About nine similar examples are known, all from the Sassari district. At Orrida (Sennori) the forecourt is again made in the rock face, but this time it opens into a built stone passage through a rock⁄cut door with a relief moulding above, reproducing the motif frequently found on the portal stones. At Mura Iddari (Abbasanta) a rock⁄cut dromos precedes a passage of Giants' Tomb type built with upright slabs.

Fig. 22

An interesting and hitherto unique plan is that of the tomb of Ottosoddos (Osidda), where the passage terminates in a wider, cist-like structure. This seems to be a freak feature like the division across the passage at Perdalunga (Austis) and need not be claimed as representing a phase of evolution from dolmen to Giants' Tomb.

Both the length of the passage and the size of the tomb may vary very considerably, as can be seen in the figure on the opposite page. Only 2 metres long at S. Giovanni (Guspini), the passage at Sas Prigionas (Bultei) extended for 10 metres, which seems about average, while in one of the two examples at Goronna, where two tombs and a nuraghe are found together on a little rocky plateau near Paulilatino, the passage was nearly 18 metres long.

Occasionally the passage may be slightly boat-shaped or widened in the middle. One such was found at S'Azzica (Abbasanta), built with some sophistication suggesting a relatively late date when compared with another at Su Cotzu de Sas Molas (Paulilatino) built in a slab construction: the feature may perhaps have no chronological significance. It is, however, reminiscent of the Minorcan *navetas*, and the two islands certainly shared other cultural affinities.

Side niches for offerings or for placing lamps are sometimes found in the burial passage. Domu S'Orcu (Siddi) and Sas Prigionas (Bultei) both have one niche, while at Scusorgiu there were pairs set one above the other. At Noazza, near the station at Birori, a tomb has two niches side by side on each wall just inside the entrance. It is interesting to note that at Regolini Galassi and other seventh-century Etruscan tombs, similar niches are found.

The burial passage itself was frequently paved either with slabs or cobbles, and may contain a large number of burials. Sixty were recorded from Las Plassas, about 30 from Scusorgiu, and about 50 from Preganti (Gergei), while at Pedra Lada

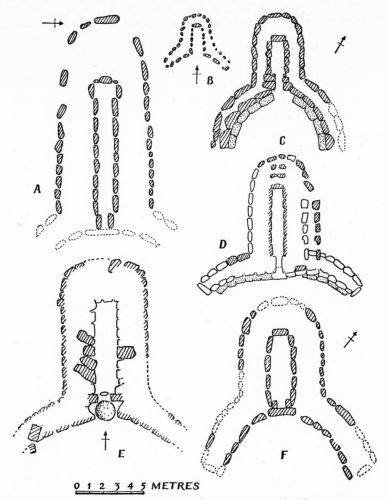

Fig. 23. Plans of various Giants' Tombs: (a) Ottosodos (Osidda); (b) S. Giovanni (Guspini); (c) Sos Ossastros (Abbasanta); (d) S'Azzica (Abbasanta); (e) Las-plassas; (f) Fontana Morta (Sorgono). (a-c, f after Mackenzie, d after Taramelli)

(Ozieri) dozens of skeletons were found all along the passage. These burials are inhumations, and sometimes included children. The numbers suggest that the life of the tombs was very long.

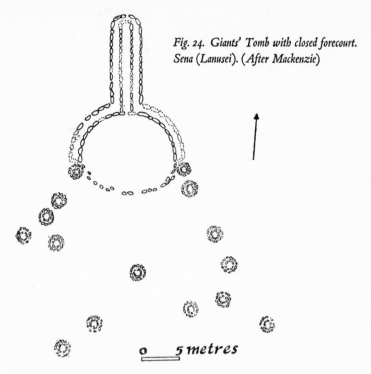

Fig. 24. Giants' Tomb with closed forecourt. Sena (Lanusei). (After Mackenzie)

o   5 metres

Occasionally we find a hint of the fertility cult practised by the builders of these tombs. At Perdu Cossu (Norbello) two blocks of stone were found in the passage, one showed a woman's breast in relief, and the other, found in situ at the end of the passage, bore a phallic relief. More usually these are found outside the tomb in the forecourt.

The outside of the tombs is often too ruined for the method of construction to be observed: some are roughly built, others made with carefully coursed masonry, and others again with polygonal construction resting on a coursed plinth, as at Srighidanu (Bauladu).

The forecourt is a feature which evidently played a con‑ siderable role in the ritual activities carried out when a burial was put into the tomb. So far these sacred areas have not been

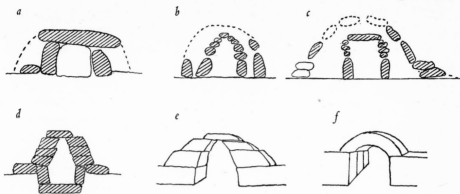

Fig. 25. Sections of Giants' Tombs, to show the different methods of construction: (a) Su Coveccu (Bultei); (b) Muraguadu (Bauladu); (c) Srighidanu (Bauladu); (d) Biristeddu (Dorgali); (e) Sas Presones (Cuglieri); (f) Pedras Doladas (Scanu Montiferru). (a-c after Mackenzie; d after Taramelli; and e, f after Pes)

given the attention they deserve, and the complete stripping of one would be rewarding for the light it would throw on the ritual practices. Offerings were evidently placed on the ledge or bench sometimes found flanking the arms of the forecourt, for example at Sos Ozzastros and S'Azzica (Ab-basanta); or they may have been put in the small pits in the forecourt area, if these did not serve for libations. In the tomb of Las Plassas a large offering pit was found in the centre of the entrance. In some instances the forecourt seems to have played an unusually important role, and the flanking arms were continued round to enclose a circular *temenos*. This was the case at San Giovanni (Guspini), Maura Pittau (Las Plassas) and Sena (Lanusei), and at the last-mentioned tomb a number of small stone structures, each about 2 metres across outside, were found near the forecourt area. They have no recorded parallel elsewhere, but may each have contained a burial.

Fig. 24

Sometimes baetylic stones were placed in the forecourt, and some of these bear carved bosses or breasts, or hollows thought

Fig. 26

to represent the same. At Sas Perdas Marmuradas, Tamuli (Macomer) there were six conical stones with breasts in relief; these were placed both behind and in front of the Giants' Tomb. At Perda Pes (Paulilatino) two conical stones with hollow 'breasts' can be seen, one of these stones having six cavities. At Goronna, one of the few tombs to have been excavated, La Marmora recorded a small conical baetyl built into the forecourt at the side of the portal stone. A similar conical baetyl was found at one of the nuragic springs, Fontana Padenti de Baccai (Lanusei), dated from finds to the eighth–sixth centuries BC. Other examples include five near a tomb at Silanus and five near one at Bonorva. Phallic symbols also occur, sometimes represented by a long groove at the top of a rounded baetyl, but these are rare. One example came from Sa Pedra e S'Altare (Silanus).

The earliest Giants' Tombs in all probability had a simple doorway closed with a slab, but many of them have a carefully cut portal stone with a small archway in the lower part to give access to the interior of the tomb. This was sometimes so small that a grown person could hardly enter. Perhaps it was used more for inserting offerings, and when new burials were admitted the whole portal stone may have been lowered. Some of these monumental stones are very imposing, and may reach a height of over 3 metres. The top of the stone is curved to correspond with the curve of the roof above the passage capstones when these were present, and the stone frequently has a raised moulding around the outside and across the centre above the port-hole, reproducing, as it were, the line of the roof and of the capstones covering the passage. Ideally this stone was made of one slab, but examples of two or three superimposed slabs are recorded. Particularly common in the uplands to the north of the Tirso valley near Paulilatino and Macomer, such imposing stones must often have been robbed for building stone, and may once have been commoner

Fig. 26. Façade of tomb at Goronna, showing monumental closing slab flanked by baetylic stones. (After La Marmora)

in other parts of the island. At the tomb of Preganti (Gergei) the port-hole had been carefully sealed up with small cubic blocks.

At the Tomba del Re, Biristeddu (near Dorgali) an ex-   Plate 29
tremely sophisticated Giants' Tomb, two carefully shaped, cut stones can be seen in the forecourt area. These were perhaps baetyls or they may have had a place in a monumental façade. These surely reflect Phoenician influence and may belong to the seventh century or so. In the same tomb one can see a stone at the end of the passage, which is cut in a curve above and which is grooved horizontally and obliquely to receive not only the last capstone covering the passage, but also the inclining stones above it. Behind this stone are several others, also rounded but of diminishing heights corresponding with the sloping end of the tomb.

At Pedras Doladas (Scano Montiferro) four monolithic arches made of simple curved stones covered the entrance into   *Fig. 25f*
the passage. Similar arches were observed at the sacred well of Su Tempiesu (Orune) and at one of the Serra Orrios temples

Plate 42

near Dorgali. These buildings are thought to belong to about the sixth century BC. Other signs of Punic or classical in, fluence are not rare. A dentellated pattern found on the portal stones of the tombs at Oragiana (Cuglieri) and at Nela (Sindìa) recall examples on Phrygian tombs, and may be contemporary with the Ionic expansion of the seventh and sixth centuries BC, though unlikely to be before the sixth century here.

More or less contemporary may be an unusual tomb, Bruncu Espis (Arbus). This, instead of being a more sophis, ticated rendering of a Giants' Tomb is a very simplified one. The façade is quite straight, without any forecourt, and the pass, age made with coursed stones, inclining inwards and once slab, covered. Punic influence is apparent from the squared angles and the quality of the stonework. The finds included an engraved bronze armlet, and the pottery, though mostly not closely datable, included a jug similar to some from Phase C (Nuragic I Upper) at Barumini, suggesting a date between the eighth and sixth centuries. There were also high strip handles recalling Carthaginian ones from Tharros and Nora, not earlier than the seventh century. Other, even simpler tombs, which may or may not be related to the Giants' Tombs, are discussed on pp. 100–103.

Many of the Giants' Tombs continued in use until very late, and it is not unusual to find even Roman sherds, suggesting their re,use or even uninterrupted use into the third century BC. Evidence for accurate dating is, however, almost absent.

Fig. 21

At Mesu Enas, the site, as we have already said, of a hybrid tomb consisting of a megalithic dromos leading into a rock, cut tomb, obsidian flakes and a triangular arrowhead were found with nuragic type pottery identical with pottery from a near,by dolmen.

Other recorded finds include bronze daggers, spearheads, swords (at least one of the very long votive swords came from a

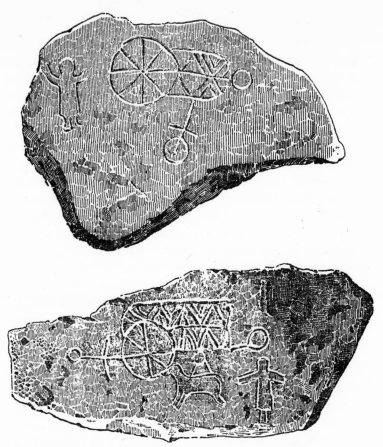

Fig. 27. *Incised stones from Giants' Tombs at Rio di Palmas, nr Sulcis*

Giants' Tomb), stone and bronze axes, big bronze pins, votive ship-lamps, bronze rings, chains and pendants, as well as bronze statuettes; and one tomb at Sallule (Urzulei) contained a double looped palstave of Huelva type. All of these fall within the long Nuragic period and, as we have stressed, although it is possible to date them more closely individually, we do not know whether they were primary or secondary in the tombs.

At Goronna, a tomb already mentioned was excavated

Fig. 27

many years ago and yielded pottery of Bonnanaro type and an obsidian arrowhead. But Bonnanaro pottery, while beginning in pre-nuragic times, continued in use for a long time, and Lilliu has suggested a date for this tomb in the period between the eighth and sixth centuries for at least one phase, while emphasising that it may have begun much earlier.

A very interesting discovery was made at a Giants' Tomb at Rio di Palmas near Sulcis, where a group of over 40 tombs were found in the alluvial plain, close to a nuraghe. One of these had a turned-over architrave at the entrance, decorated with an incised drawing of people and a wheeled vehicle, perhaps a coffer like the bronze model from Oschiri, shown in plate 64. A short distance away in the probable remains of another tomb, a second incised stone was found. Stylistically somewhat similar to the well-known Val Camonica series, they may date from about the seventh century B C, and analogies of the same date may perhaps be found in some of the Picene stelae from near Pesaro.

A very recent excavation in the Arzachena district of the Gallura has not yet been published in detail but promises to be of great value. Here a Giants' Tomb has had a secondary passage built back to back with the original passage, but at a higher level and sharing the same end slab. The pottery sequence from this important excavation is eagerly awaited and it is said to include much 'Bronze Age' ware.

MISCELLANEOUS LONG CISTS

Possibly related to the Giants' Tombs but different in both plan and construction are some tombs known as 'Poliandro tombs' on account of the numerous burials they contain; these are, in fact, long cist-like graves, rectangular or trapeze-shaped. Some of these fall within the Nuragic period and share a few features with the Giants' Tombs. Others may be pre-nuragic, and it is possible that some developed from the oval, stone-revetted tomb of Settimo San Pietro type, described on p. 70, or the tombs found at San Gemiliano (Sestu), or Sa Duchessa.

Three tombs called at the time of their discovery '*a cassone*' tombs came to light at Domusnovas Canales in the Tirso valley in 1915, but they were not, unfortunately, published in detail. They are reported as having been close to some dolmens, and to have contained 'Bronze Age' pottery. Two were rectangular and one roughly oval with seven big orthostatic slabs on each side. Near by was the Nuraghe Nurarchei.

At San Giuliano near Alghero a recently discovered, and as yet not fully published, tomb was found. It was lined with dry stone walling and contained remains of about 54 individuals, as well as a carinated cup and other pottery, and some copper awls or netting needles of Anghelu Ruju type.

Two others at Bopitos at the foot of Monte Ultano (Laerru) may be earlier than the Giants' Tombs, though the dating evidence is very uncertain. One tomb was rectangular and built of upright slabs. A small offering pit full of carbonised material was found at the entrance, and inside the tomb were the remains of four bodies thought to have been placed in a sitting position. The grave goods were rough sherds, not closely datable. The second tomb was boat-shaped and contained at least ten persons, the grave goods including a little bowl with four small lugs below the rim, and a lid with a handle.

Fig. 28

At Ena'e Muros (Ossi) excavations were carried out in a trapeze-shaped tomb, made with large, carefully cut, flat slabs. It contained over 30 skeletons, some crouched and others extended. A quantity of pottery was also recovered including part of a tripod with concave sectioned foot (of Monte Claro rather than Nuragic affinity) and one sherd with applied cordons (a form of decoration also present on some Monte Claro pots); Bonnanaro ware was also represented. There were also two oval flat bronze daggers, each with two rivets in a

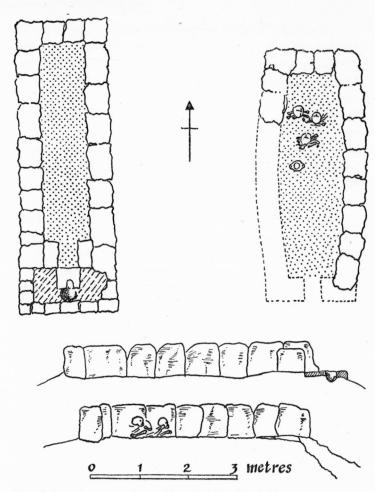

Fig. 28. Long cist graves at Bopitos (Laerru). (After Taramelli)

rounded butt; a type which, beginning early, had a long time span. The tomb cannot yet, therefore, be closely dated, but Contu suggests it belongs to the early Nuragic period.

Another trapeze-shaped tomb was found at Nerbonis (Gesturi). It was lined with dry stone walling and had rectangular niches or 'loculi' along the sides, arranged in pairs one over the other, recalling a similar arrangement at the Giants' Tomb at Scusorgiu. The passage or chamber was covered with three thin stone slabs. Many bones were recovered, but there is again no dating evidence.

Near the temple of Sant'Anastasia (Sardara) a tomb which seems to have been rather similar was found in 1914, but no plan of it was made. Lined with courses of inclined stones, it contained the remains of many persons, including some which evidently had been partially burnt. All these skeletons lay on a paved floor which had apparently been covered with a thin sheet of bronze. Two bronze statuettes of archers reveal a full nuragic date.

To approximately the same date or only slightly later belongs a single-burial tomb at Senorbì. Lined with slabs covered with a capstone, it contained a male inhumation with a long, hilted bronze sword and some rivetted bronze sheeting with a handle. Taramelli suggested that this may have been part of a breastplate, but it is not very convincing. The form of the sword recalls some of the daggers from the Teti (Abini) hoard.

Fig. 53

Lastly, attention must be drawn to a tomb excavated in recent years at Motrox'e Bois (Usellus). The rectangular chamber was paved with flagstones, and the walls built with obliquely cut stones, once probably inclining inwards to join over the chamber, and recalling the stonework at the Giants' Tomb at Biristeddu and some of the sacred wells. About 20 to 25 skeletons were found to have been disturbed in ancient times, and one part of the tomb had a secondary level pointing to its re-use. Several sherds of a brownish carinated bowl, probably of late nuragic affinities, came from this tomb, as well as small objects of ivory, bone and amber, some probably Punic glass beads, copper armlets (one with herring-bone decoration), etc. A votive stiletto of iron with a steatite handle

Fig. 25d

has analogies from Tharros, and iron stilettos were also found in the Forraxi Nioi hoard and elsewhere. The excavator suggests that the earliest phase is unlikely to ante-date the eighth century, while the secondary use of the tomb, indicated by some burnt bones, probably belonged to the fourth century B C.

Many of these tombs, being below the surface, will only come to light slowly in the course of time. Sporadic use of single cist-burials seem to have started with Li Muri, Arzachena, and continued into the period of Carthaginian occupation. But what underlay the choice of this kind of burial when a clear alternative was often present in rock-cut tombs, Giants' Tombs or 'dolmens', we do not yet know. Nor do we know whether the long, collective, cists were related to the Giants' Tombs. Only time and more excavations will give us the answer.

STANDING STONES AND STONE SETTINGS

Some 50 standing stones still exist in Sardinia, and no doubt a great many more have been destroyed or remain undiscovered. Lilliu, who made a list of them complete up to 1957, recorded ten from the province of Sassari, 13 from Cagliari, and the majority, 27, from the province of Nuoro. Of these, 31 are isolated examples, and there are 13 instances where the stones were found in pairs, and six groups of three.

One of a pair at Genna Prunas has ten holes arranged in a triangle, but most of these stones are simple, varying in the amount of dressing, in the type of stone (though usually granite or basalt) and in dimensions. Some are small and may be less than 1 metre high, while others are known which reach a height of 9 metres.

The function of these stones was certainly not always the same: some were tombstones, others cenotaphs, while others again were just territorial boundary stones.

Close dating is not possible, but it seems likely that the practice of setting up standing stones went back to the Bronze and maybe even to the Copper Age. Some have been found near Copper Age sites or near rock-cut tombs, and one must remember that the large idol of so-called Cycladic type at Senorbì was evidently set up in the first place in the ground, and differs from the small portable type known from Anghelu Ruju and contemporary sites. The unusual tomb group at Li Muri, near Arzachena, too, shows that standing stones formed an integral part of the burial site, which dates back certainly to before the mid-second millennium, if not considerably before. Others are found near the Giants' Tombs and La Marmora speaks of several instances, for example Goronna and Perda Pes (Paulilatino), where the stones were placed in a ring before the tombs. These standing stones seem to have survived in use through the Nuragic period, even, according to Pope Gregory, into Christian times, for he complained of the Sardinians that *ligna autem et lapides adorent*.

Fig. 3

Plate 30

Stone circles are also recorded. One was found surrounding a standing stone at Maioiada (Nuoro), and a megalithic circle was claimed at Domusnovas Canales. At Perdalunga a circular paved area had three standing stones in the centre, and Gouin found other stone settings in the Abbasanta region. Some of these settings may be related to the sites near Li Muri, Arzachena, only recently excavated and not yet fully published. Here the remains look like circular huts with well-marked doorways and a tall central pillar; they are thought to belong to the Copper Age. These sites in the Gallura may have been connected culturally with Corsica, though statue menhirs of typically Corsican type are not represented in Sardinia.

CHAPTER IV

The Nuragic Culture: Buildings

THE NURAGHI

THE MOST CHARACTERISTIC and interesting of all the Sardinian monuments are the nuraghi. About 6,500 of these conical towers, some complex and well preserved, others simple, and often robbed down to the footings, can still be seen today; many others still remain to be identified among the forests and rocks.

There are various divergent forms of the name nuraghe (*nuraxi, nuraki,* etc.) which is thought to belong to an early, pre-Indo-European linguistic tradition. It has two meanings, 'heap' or 'hollow', either of which could apply equally well. On the other hand the Siciliot Greeks thought that the nuraghi were built and named after Norax, founder of Nora. Certainly by the fourth century BC the term nuraghe was already known to the Greeks.

Fig. 29

Nuraghi are found all over the island and in all types of terrain, but their greatest concentration is round the upland plateaux to the north of the Tirso river (the Marghine), in the Nurra and around Sassari, and in the central south (the Trexenta) around what is perhaps the most well-known of all the nuraghi, Barumini, excavated by Lilliu in recent years. Of course in fertile land like the Campidano which has been farmed for thousands of years, others have no doubt been dismantled for building stone so that the distribution pattern of today only partially reflects the original one. Mostly built at an altitude of between 200 and 700 metres above sea level, there are rare examples at even 1,000 metres.

Their rather more westerly distribution results from several factors: the richest farming land was here, and land more easily adapted for habitation before the forests had been extensively cleared; here, too, were the natural harbours sought by the Phoenician and Punic settlers, against whom the nuragic peoples set up their defences at points of vantage; and here were most of the foreign markets, within range of which, in times of relative peace, the local people lived and traded. The Nuragic chieftains, too, lording over territories which fluctuated continually in size and richness depending on natural resources and on success in inter-tribal warfare, placed their own nuraghi and those of their dependants in advantageous positions. All these local and temporary exigencies are re-flected in the distribution pattern as we see it today. We can imagine the various defensive necessities of both families and larger, tribal, units; but we may never be able to separate and identify the individual groups within the whole. We may, however, surmise that the nuraghi crowded around Olbia were built there for trading rather than defensive reasons, for many of them are in low-lying and strategically untenable positions. So, too, the carefully sited and systematically grouped nuraghi along parts of the coast which were open to Phoenicio-Punic landings presumably represented a deliberate defensive disposition planned by the coastal tribes. Again in the Trexenta and elsewhere, some of the *giare*, or plateaux, are ringed all round the crest with nuraghi which evidently guarded the marshy upland ranches from cattle thieves.

Many other nuraghi may have been simply farmhouses belonging to individual families who when threatened retired into one of the large, well-defended nuraghi which by the Full Nuragic period were so evolved that, surrounded with outer towers, curtain walls and redoubts, they are estimated in some cases to have had a garrison of as many as 200–300 men armed with spears, swords, bows or slings. Such strength indicates an organised community acting under the direction of a war-lord.

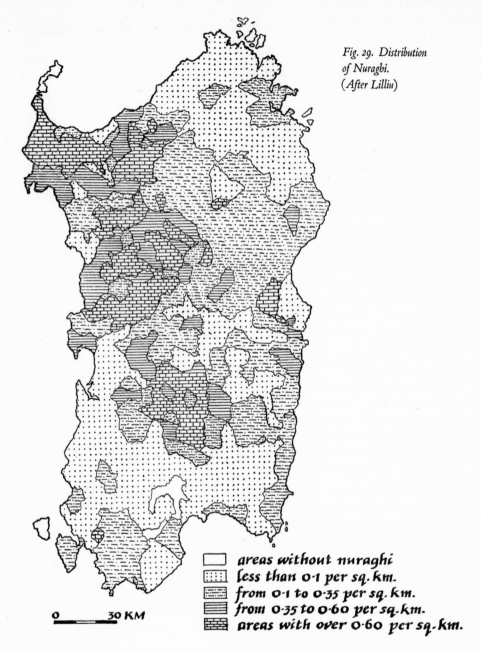

Fig. 29. Distribution
of Nuraghi.
(After Lilliu)

☐ areas without nuraghi
▦ less than 0·1 per sq. km.
▦ from 0·1 to 0·35 per sq. km.
▦ from 0·35 to 0·60 per sq. km.
▦ areas with over 0·60 per sq. km.

0   30 KM

The tradition of building round or oval houses was, as we have seen, a long-established one in Sardinia; the vaulted roof which is found in the classic nuraghi, may, however, have been introduced from outside, from the Mycenaean world perhaps, which we know was linked to the western Mediter-ranean at least by trade contacts soon after the mid second millennium. Sardinia was not, as far as we know, much affected by this trade, unlike the Lipari islands and Sicily, but some contacts are shown by the Cypriot copper ingots from several sites in the island. These may have been shipped by Mycenaean or Phoenician traders, and they help us to date the early nuraghi near which they were found.

The dating of the earliest nuraghi has not yet been ascer-tained from excavation, but there are three factors which, together, indicate a date of about 1400 BC for the simplest archaic form.

When discussing the Monte Claro culture, we drew atten-tion to the new and as yet unpublished excavations at Sa Corona, Villagreca, where a megalithic hut which may be related to the most archaic type of nuraghe, was associated with pottery likely to date from approximately the fourteenth century. It has also been pointed out that at the sacred site of Monte D'Accoddi, the technical skill for building with over-lapping stones to diminish the diameter of the monument only lacked the 'idea' of the tholos to make such a construction practicable. This idea may have originated locally by copying the clay-daubed timber roof in stone; it is more probable, however, that the Sardinian peoples may have heard of, or even seen, some of the big tholos tombs of the Mycenaean world or the similar structural methods used in the side chambers of the Maltese temples.

The second significant factor for dating the early nuraghi comes from Barumini, one of the largest of the complex examples of the Trexenta. Here, in the earliest nucleus of the building, a piece of timber was recovered which has been dated by Carbon 14 analysis to 1470±200 years (not 1270± 200 years as originally published). The latest date (about 1270) is perhaps archaeologically the most acceptable, especially as the earliest element at Barumini is typologically not quite the most archaic type of tower, for reasons which will be discussed below.

Lastly, we have the evidence from the copper ingots associ-ated with some archaic nuraghi which have not yet been excavated. Five ox-hide type ingots were found near a nuraghe at Serra Ilixi, Nuragus. Three of these were well preserved and bore inscribed Minoan signs or founder's marks. Another was found a few metres away from a nuraghe at Sant'Antioco, Bisarcio, in the Ozieri district (again inscribed with a Minoan sign), and another at Assemini.

Plate 31

The dating of these ingots has oscillated between about 1500 and 1050 BC. They were discussed by Schaeffer who attri-buted their arrival in Sardinia to the Land and Sea Raiders of the Eastern Mediterranean in about 1200–1050. Lilliu, dis-agreeing with Schaeffer, drew attention again to the analogies between the Sardinian ingots and those from, *inter alia*, Haghia Triada in Crete and other Mycenaean and Cypriot examples, emphasising that Haghia Triada was destroyed in the late fourteenth century. He supported his plea for an earlier dating by pointing out that analogous ingots are carved on the Egyptian tomb of the vizier Rekhmire in the reign of Thothmes III in 1445 or so. He proposed a date of about 1400 for the ingots which were presumably received at already existing nuraghi, founded perhaps in the fifteenth century, while some earlier nuraghi near the coast (such as the Nuraghe sa Domu s'Orcu) may go back to the sixteenth century. More recently Buchholz has stressed that the Sardinian ingots find their closest analogies in the Cypriot examples, not earlier than the fourteenth century. Whereas all types are shown on the

Egyptian tombs, the Cypriot type is found only once on the Greek mainland, and not at all in Crete, though one of Sardinian type was found in Crete where it may belong to the thirteenth-twelfth centuries.

Recently we have been fortunate in obtaining an even closer dating. In a submarine excavation carried out in 1960 off the Turkish coast at Gelidonya, the cargo of a wreck included forty ox-hide ingots, together with bun ingots, pottery, scarabs, and implements of various kinds. The ingots are of three different forms, all of which fall within Buchholz's Type II, and two of the forms are analogous to the ingots from Serra Ilixi. The scarabs are said to be almost certainly of the XIXth Egyptian Dynasty; the shapes of the implements seem to be Cypriot, and so do the founder's marks on the ingots, for similar marks are found on pottery both from Cyprus itself and from the Cypriot colony of Ras Shamra in Syria. Whether this ship was Cypriot, Syrian or Helladic need not concern us here, but it is important that she is thought to have foundered around 1200 BC. Thus Schaeffer's argument seems vindicated.

The general inference which can be drawn from these three pieces of evidence is that the earliest nuragic houses or archaic nuraghi may have slowly developed from about 1400 BC (perhaps a little later than Lilliu's proposed date), allowing a period of about a hundred years for the evolution to reach the Barumini stage which cannot, on the Carbon 14 evidence, be later than 1270 BC. By about 1200 the inhabitants of the archaic nuraghi were receiving copper ingots (some of which weigh over 300 kilograms, about 750 lb., and had a considerable value) from traders coming from the East Mediterranean who may also have inspired the first *tholos* roofs. These traders have not yet been identified, but there is certainly a possibility that they were the Land and Sea Raiders, including the so-called Shardana who may have given their name to Sardinia. This problem will be briefly discussed in another chapter.

Plate 32

There are two main classes of nuraghi: first, the classic nuraghe with corbelled vault or *tholos* roofing to the chambers, and second a degenerate, or possibly archaic, building resem- bling the classic type in certain respects, but having slab- covered corridors or galleries inside in place of the vaulted chamber.

The earliest of the classic nuraghi were probably only one storey high, built on a prepared platform, in the shape of a truncated cone. No mortar was used, and the big blocks were built in courses in diminishing circles to obtain the required height and shape. Inside was one room only, vaulted above and closed at the top with one or more slabs. Sometimes a terrace above was reached by an interior stair (at first, perhaps, a movable rope or wooden ladder), and later a stone-built stair which in the earliest examples led out of the round or oval chamber, and subsequently from the entrance corridor. For defensive purposes this stair was often deliberately discontinu- ous, so that the enemy, groping in the semi-darkness, had to search for the continuation. At the same time the chamber was provided with niches, probably for beds, in the thickness of the wall, near ground level (as, for example, at Barumini). The outer walls of the most archaic nuraghi seem to have been more sharply inclined, and the *tholos* roof to the chamber higher in relation to its diameter than in the later examples. The entrance passage, too, reveals a simple evolution from those in which the roof joins the main tower at an obtuse angle, to the later ones in which this junction is at right-angles. The provision not only of a stair leading from it, but often of a guard-chamber as well, becomes increasingly common. More storeys were also added above.

All these simple forms of nuraghi fall within the Archaic Nuragic period which we may date approximately 1400–950 BC. Into this period we should place Sa Corona, followed by Sa Domu S'Orcu (Sarrok), the earliest phase at Barumini,

Sant' Antioco and Serra Ilixi, and perhaps the nuraghi such as Enna Pruna, Su Guventu, and others which are associated with Monte Claro ware. Another development which seems to belong to the latter part of the Archaic Nuragic period is revealed in a few examples where a strong sheathing wall has *Fig. 30e* been built all round the nuraghe, either to its full height or to the height of the terrace; a feature which finds its exact counter' part at Balestra and other *torre* in Corsica. Both Balestra and Foce, which very closely resemble the Sardinian nuraghe of Murartu (Silanus) and Sa Coa Filigosa (Bolotana), are regarded by Grosjean, their excavator, as tombs; but this attribution is still uncertain.

By the Full or Middle Nuragic period (about 950-500 BC) *Fig. 30-31f-o* the social pattern was changing. Sea'borne traffic was increas' ing rapidly, and Sardinia was in touch with many parts of the Mediterranean. The greater wealth resulting from Phoenician trade and the development of metalworking called for greater security. Even before the advent of the Phoenician establish' ments on the coast, response to these changes in wealth is reflected in a sudden acceleration in the nuraghe's evolution leading to more and more variety in plan and ever'increasing sophistication. Frontal or lateral outworks were added, and sometimes the whole complex was then enclosed with walling, as at Palmavera not far from Alghero, where this phase can be dated from bronze objects to about 750 BC. Others had additional towers linked to the original one, and according to

Fig. 30-31 (overleaf). Plans of Nuraghi: (a) Orrubiu (Arzana); (b) S'Iscala e Pedra (Semestene); (c) Genna Masoni (Gairo); (d) Tittiriola (Bolotana); (e) Sa Coa Filigosa (Bolotana); (f) Molineddu (Seneghe); (g) Palmavera (Alghero); (h) Mont'e S'Orku Tueri (Perdasdefogu); (i) Sa Mura e Mazzala (Scanu Montiferru); (j) Nuracc'e Deu (Gesturi); (k) Santa Sofia (Guspini); (l) Noddule (Nuoro); (m) Pranu Nuracci (Siris); (n) Losa (Abbasanta), (see also fig. 36); (o) Santa Barbara (Macomer); (p) Orribiu (Orroli), (see also fig. 38); (q) Sa Domu e S'Orku (Ortu) Domusnovas; (r) Su Nuraxi (Barumini), (see also figs. 34 and 35). (All except e after Lilliu)

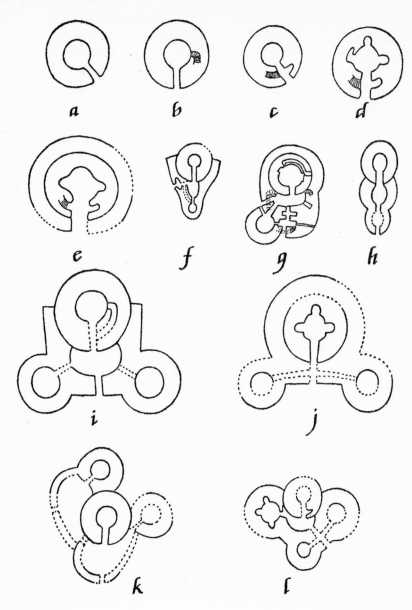

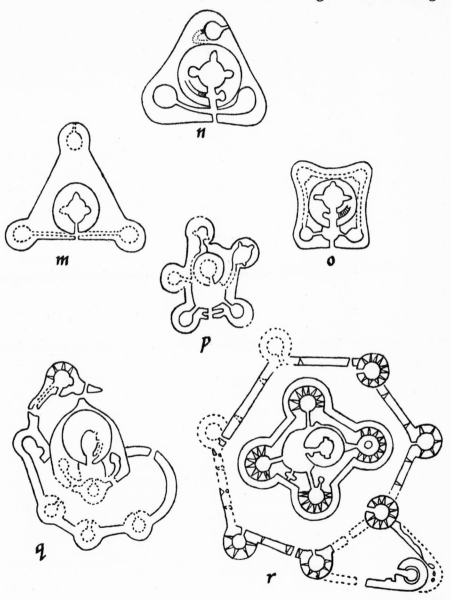

n

m

o

p

q

r

the number of these towers the nuraghi are described as bilobate, trilobate, etc. These outer towers were sometimes linked with straight, and sometimes with sinuous walling, and from finds of pottery and bronze in the courtyards at Losa, Lugherras and Sant'Antine, this development can be dated at least as early as the eighth century.

The tower of the original nuraghe was sometimes crowned with a jutting parapet supported on corbels. This was neces-sary to overcome the dangers caused by having dead ground near the base of the sloping walls. At first these parapets were almost certainly made of wood, but the later ones were prob-ably stone-built. Evidence for them is provided not only from the nuraghi themselves, from Losa and Barumini where stone corbels were found in the filling of the courtyard below, but also from small models of nuraghi such as those found at Olmedo and Barumini belonging to the seventh–sixth centuries. Another model from Ittireddu shows a flat top to

Plate 33

the towers, with no indication of a fighting platform, the lack of which seriously detracts from its defensive nature.

The great multi-towered nuraghi which mark the fully evolved defensive architecture of just before the Carthaginian invasion in the late sixth century, were designed to withstand

Fig. 31p–r

new forms of warfare including various siege-engines and battering rams and large quantities of projectiles have been found near some of them. A massive wall was added round the central complex; the entrance was sometimes placed high up in the walling, reached only by portable ladders, and wells were sunk in the courtyards to provide a water supply in times of prolonged siege. It is interesting, too, that the splaying of the lighting- or arrow-slits narrowed towards the outside of the wall, in contrast to medieval loopholes which are designed to cover as much ground outside as possible; and one cannot help wondering whether this arrangement may not have been deliberately devised to overcome the danger of being smoked out by the enemy. It allowed less space for them to thrust in burning faggots and straw, and more space for the besieged to fight the fires.

At Barumini, Lilliu has recognised two phases which fall within this Full Nuragic period. He has called them Nuragic I Lower, which dates to about the tenth–eighth centuries on the basis of pottery analogies both with the Italian mainland and with the lingering Monte Claro tradition, and Nuragic I Upper (mid eighth–sixth centuries) which produced pottery forms such as the oblique-mouthed jug, or *Schnabelkanne*, which find analogies from the well temple at Sant'Anastasia, and from Pantalica in Sicily. A number of other nuraghi have produced bronzes of this phase: an *a navicella* brooch of the seventh century from Barumini, and many swords, daggers, bronze statuettes, etc., from others.

Fig. 34

These great forts with their clustered huts outside, their towers, curtain walls, parapets, terraces and massive central keep rising above all the outworks, are surely among the most impressive monuments remaining to us in prehistoric Europe. As one gropes through the ill-lit passages and up the flights of steps within the thickness of the walls, one cannot feel other than amazement at the immense strength of the buildings and at the military ingenuity of the people who devised and constructed them. Only the enormous experience and man-power of the Carthaginian army could lead to their fall.

Fig. 34
Plate 39

In the Late Nuragic period (500–238 BC) nuraghi con-tinued to be built in parts of the island outside the area of Carthaginian domination, and even within that area many of them continued, no doubt, to be occupied. Some of the nuraghi built at this time belong to the second group which, while sharing certain features with the classic nuraghi (con-struction in coursed blocks, staircase, etc.), are really much less sophisticated buildings. It has been suggested that these gallery (or corridor or hide-out) nuraghi, some 30 or so of

Fig. 32

which are known today, resulted from a different building tradition, more markedly western (like the dolmens) than the classic type which, at least in some of its characteristics, was inspired from the Eastern Mediterranean. The plan of the gallery nuraghi varies from one to another, but the internal passages, deliberately ill-lit and often doubling back at a sharp angle, are found in place of the round or oval chamber. The intention seems to have been to confuse anyone entering for hostile purposes, and to enable the defenders to pounce on the attackers as they groped in the darkness. The hypothesis, supported by Lilliu, that these nuraghi were late and degenerate is convincing for the majority of them, and he refers them to the period of guerilla warfare first against the Carthaginians and then against the Romans. Diodorus Siculus, quoting from information taken from Timaeus in the fourth century BC, and Pausanias writing of the Roman campaign of 231 BC both speak of the natives taking refuge in 'underground constructions' or 'caves'. In fact, most of these gallery nuraghi are found in places where they could easily be concealed among the rocks or woods, and their design is reminiscent of the souterrains of the Roman period in Scotland, or those in Ireland, though these, as the name implies, were always underground. Describing them, Diodorus says that 'the Iolaes fled for safety to the mountainous parts of the island, and built underground dwellings, and here they raised many flocks and herds which supplied them with food in abundance, so that they were able to maintain themselves on a diet of milk, and cheese and meat.' He may also have heard of the great limestone refuge of Monte Tiscali, described on page 145.

Such a late dating for the gallery nuraghi was challenged recently by Contu who regarded them as archaic rather than degenerate. His excavations at Peppe Gallu revealed an occupation immediately underlying a Punic level, and though one might argue from the simple pottery forms that the site

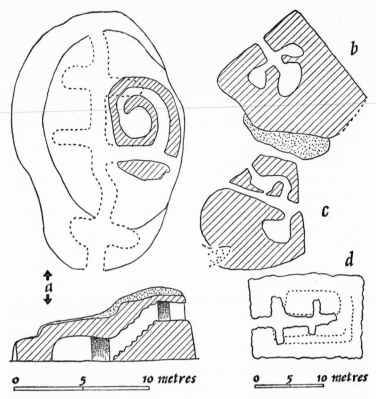

Fig. 32. Gallery or corridor nuraghi: (a) Nuraghe Tusari (after Cherchi); (b) Tanca Manna (after Manconi); (c) Agnu (after Manconi); (d) Fonte e Mola (after Taramelli)

could have been either early or late, a Carbon 14 dating of the sixth–fourth centuries B C supports the latter probability.

Two other nuraghi of this class, Fronte Mola (Thiesi) and Albucciu (Arzachena), have been partly excavated, but the finds are not yet published, though the latter produced a bronze statuette (seventh century?), a gamma-hilted dagger and pottery which included a Punic painted vase.

But the truth is, perhaps, that some of these nuraghi may be early – contemporary, that is to say, with the archaic nuraghi of classic type – and others late. For in Corsica a structure at

Filitosa which is closely comparable to the Sardinian gallery nuraghi has been dated by Carbon 14 analysis to 1193±105 BC, and the two islands can hardly have had entirely independ-ent developments. In Corsica there are other comparable sites, some of which (for example, Torre) might be as late as the seventh–sixth centuries or even later, to judge by the pottery. One cannot therefore rule out the possibility that some of the nuraghi and *torre* were early in origin, but that others were the 'underground structures' of the classical writers. Further excavations will, no doubt, clarify this point.

While differing in many details, the generic resemblance of many Corsican *torre* both to gallery and classic nuraghi in Sardinia is undeniable. In the Balearics, too, there are *talayots* resembling both our types. The chronological position of these is uncertain; but Ses Païsses, which has affinities with gallery nuraghi, has been dated stratigraphically to the late second to early first millennia, and the *sesi* of Pantelleria, which are also analogous, may belong to the same period. Others, in Majorca, are mentioned by classical writers in describing the anti-Roman campaign of 122 BC, when, as in Sardinia, the indigenous peoples were hunted out of their hide-outs with the aid of police dogs.

The resemblances which we have noted between the tower-like buildings in Sardinia, Corsica and the Balearics need come as no surprise; nor need we be surprised to find that the nuraghi have certain features (for example, the rectangular chamber at Malosa near Laerru) in common with some tombs in Vetulonia. Not only were all these lands within easy navigable range of each other, but the buildings themselves, like the brochs and souterrains of Scotland, were the logical response to similar historical and geological conditions of peoples who, accustomed to building with large stones, wished to reinforce their round houses to meet the threat of more developed warfare.

But no account of the nuraghi would be complete without a short summary of some of the more interesting ones. We must, however, limit ourselves to only a few.

Near Torralba large numbers of nuraghi built of basalt are scattered over a strange countryside full of lava fields and small extinct volcanoes. By far the largest and most interesting is the Nuraghe Sant'Antine, only a few hundred metres from the station, which is on the main line between Olbia or Sassari and Cagliari. Still showing evidence of many huts and other buildings around it which have not yet been excavated, this is perhaps the most spectacular of all the nuraghi. A big central tower three storeys high belongs to the end of the ninth century, and may have been preceded by an even earlier one. Added to this in the eighth–seventh centuries were three single-roomed towers, linked by a two-storeyed corridor wall enclosing a courtyard with a well. The interior plan is complicated, and no less than seven entrances lead off the courtyard: into the main tower, into the passage surrounding it, and into the angle towers. A small Roman building of the first century B C is built against the outer wall on one side.

Plates 36, 38
Fig. 33

There may have been only a short lapse of time between the first and second building phase, and there may have been a third phase just before the destruction of the nuraghe in the Carthaginian campaign. More excavations are needed before the full history of the buildings can be worked out.

Only a little less spectacular than Sant'Antine is the nuraghe of Su Nuraxi at Barumini, the first and only nuraghe which has been scientifically excavated in recent years. It stands in undulating country in the Trexenta, and can be reached without difficulty from Cagliari (about 65 kilometres).

Figs. 31r, 34 and 35
Plates 37, 39

A huge central tower, originally about 17 metres high and built of basalt blocks, contains three superimposed *tholos* chambers. The entrance on ground level has a guard-chamber on the right, and a staircase, beginning at about $3\frac{1}{2}$ metres above ground level, opens off to the left. The date of this tower must be earlier than the ninth–eighth centuries, and if the Carbon 14 dating is correct, should go back to 1470±200 BC (the latest date of about 1270 being more probable). The ground plan of this early nuraghe has two niches or bed recesses, from which it is inferred that it is not, typologically, the most archaic type. These niches may have been lined with cork for sleeping on, as quantities of cork were found here, and in other nuraghi too.

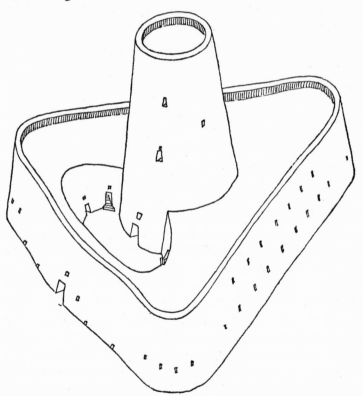

Fig. 33. Sant'Antine (Torralba). Reconstruction after Mingazzini of the second stage of construction

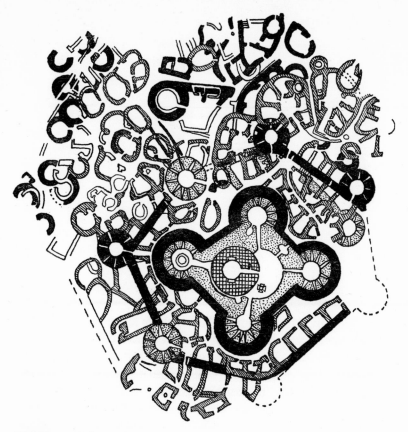

 Archaic Nuragic
Nuragic First lower
Nuragic First upper
Second Nuragic
Punico-Roman

*Fig. 34. General
plan of Barumini.
(After Lilliu)*

In the next phase of its evolution (first half of eighth century)
Su Nuraxi was provided with a four-towered addition,
enclosing the original nucleus, outside the entrance of which a
space was left for a courtyard. Some huts were also grouped
below the fortress at this time, and it was strengthened with
several free-standing towers outside.

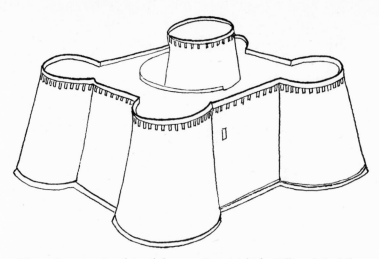

Fig. 35. Reconstruction of central element at Barumini. (After Lilliu and Crudeli)

Fig. 35

Soon after this (second half of eighth to late sixth century) the four towers and their linking walls were re-faced with a strong sheathing wall. The outer towers of the last phase were linked together with an enclosure wall punctuated at the seven angles with two of these towers and several newly constructed ones. The village outside the fortress continued to develop. This phase was brought to an abrupt and violent end when the nuraghe was besieged and then sacked by the Carthaginians at the end of the sixth century.

In the fifth century and later (Lilliu's Second Nuragic) the old village, sacked and ruined, was again occupied by the descendants of its earlier inhabitants, and this occupation lasted down into Punico-Roman times.

Fig. 36

The Nuraghe Losa is one of many nuraghi on the wide basalt plateau of Abbasanta. It stands close to the main road to Oristano, only a mile or two from Abbasanta. Here the constructional phases can be inferred only from its architec-tural features. A pottery tripod-leg of Bonnanaro type seems

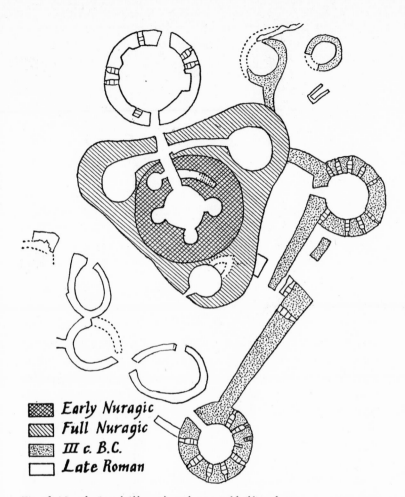

Fig. 36. Nuraghe Losa (Abbasanta), with suggested building phases

to suggest an original phase in the second millennium for the main tower, which was several storeys high. A trilobate addition was built in a second phase, probably in the Full Nuragic period, when the three towers were linked to the main keep with a level platform, and the keep itself was provided with a balcony having a parapet of shaped ashlars.

Belonging to a third phase, an outer turreted wall still remains in a good state of preservation on the north and west, and may date from the time of the Carthaginian campaign of the late sixth or early fifth century just before the nuraghe was sacked. Possibly contemporary with this turreted wall, there was a huge outer enclosing wall (also provided with several turrets) at some distance from the main buildings. More excavations are needed here before this sequence can be verified.

Plate 35,
Fig. 37

Santa Barbara at Macomer stands close to the town (a few miles from Abbasanta) on both the main railway and main road linking Sassari with Oristano and Cagliari. An early tower with niches, guard-chamber and staircase has a four-towered addition each of whose towers contains a *tholos* chamber. The whole complex is linked with a curtain wall through which the entrance passes, to continue straight across a small courtyard into the original nuraghe. These additions pre-date the late sixth century.

Nuraghe Lugherras at Paulilatino has an interesting history. An original nuraghe of several storeys was re-faced with a

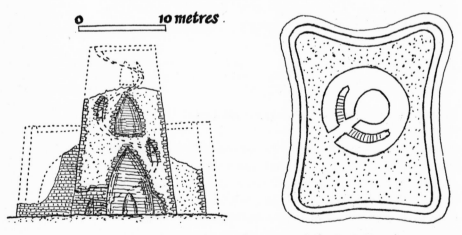

0   **10 metres** .

Fig. 37. Santa Barbara (Macomer), plan and section of upper storey. (After F. G. Newton)

trilobate addition in about the ninth–seventh centuries, and a frontal tower and a big curtain wall with four towers in the seventh–sixth centuries. After the nuraghe was dismantled by the Carthaginians, a small Punic temple was built on its summit, and the finds from the site continue into late Roman times, and include 'pilum' points of that period.

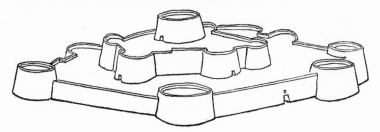

Fig. 38. Reconstruction of the latest phase of Nuraghi Orrubiu (Orroli)

Another of the particularly grandiose nuraghi is that of S'Uraki at San Vero Milis, the sequence of which, however, has yet to be worked out. The whole complex, with its big eight-towered curtain wall around it, presumably fell before the third century B C, if not earlier, at the hands of the Car- thaginians. And the great nuraghe of Orrubiu (Orroli) probably fell at about the same date.

Fig. 31p
Fig. 38

SACRED WELLS AND SPRINGS

More than once the early historians refer to the veneration of water in ancient Sardinia, and this practice can in part be explained by the serious need for water in the long dry spells which may last for several months at a stretch. But the cult connected with still or flowing water is by no means peculiar to Sardinia, even if the buildings associated with it in the island appear to be unique in character; once again we must attribute this to the individuality of the Sardinian peoples,

127

particularly around the beginning of the first millennium B C when ideas were picked up in the course of commerce with Phoenicians, Greeks, Etruscans and even perhaps return, ing Shardana, and then transmuted and developed along purely local lines. We see this happening in almost every aspect of life, artistic, architectural and religious: strange, half, understood contributions accepted in part from the more developed civilisations, redesigned to fit the local exigencies and taste.

Of the rites which took place at these sacred waters we are almost completely ignorant. We know that bronze figures of devotees, and of animals, as well as weapons and other objects of bronze, were offered to the deity here; they were placed before or at the side of the buildings covering the well or spring, for on the paved area around the well, head the stone bases, bored to hold the lead soldering for attaching the votive objects, are frequently found. That some of the waters were, and still are, medicinal and were credited with miraculous powers in Sardinia, we know from Solinus; and the idea of anointing the eyes with sacred water in order to improve the eyesight is widespread over parts of the Mediterranean, and a possible reflection of this belief can be seen in certain bronze figures with four eyes or two pupils, gratefully or hopefully offered perhaps for benefits received or solicited.

Wells and springs are distributed all over the island, but it is not always known which of them were venerated. Some, times their sacred character may only be revealed by the chance discovery of the votive deposit belonging to them, as for instance at the sanctuary at Olmedo, and even without ex, cavation one can assume with some degree of certainty that wells associated with sanctuaries were venerated.

About 20 springs belonging to the nuragic period are known, and a large number of wells, some 30 or more of which are consecrated ones. Neither springs nor wells have a limited

distribution, but are found all over the island. A very dis⁄
tinctive type of building to cover and protect the sacred waters
generally comprises three elements: the well itself, covered with
a cupola; a flight of steps leading down to the well⁄head;
and a level paved area above. The springs, which may have
been sanctified a little earlier than the majority of the wells, are
often simply cut into the hill⁄side, and tend to have a less
sophisticated superstructure. The spring at Sos Molavidos
(Orani) produced a quantity of votive material including
some tripods which may be as early as the tenth–ninth cen⁄
turies B C. On the whole, however, the exact chronological
position of these sites is difficult to fix, since, once consecrated,
they tended to remain in use for many centuries, during which
alterations took place and paving was relaid. To this day at
Nurallao in the province of Nuoro, the statue of St Peter is
carried in procession to a well, let down into it, and asked
whether or not it will rain. This sort of ultimatum to the saint
to produce rain for the crops must be a continuation of a very
early, pagan practice, only thinly disguised under the veneer
of Christianity.

The cupola covering the sacred well (or well⁄temple, it
might be called) may be above or partly above ground (some⁄
times it was evidently under a mound of earth), or it may be
completely underground. It was built with overlapping stones
which gradually reduced the diameter of what was, in fact, a
small *tholos* structure made in a technique already familiar
from the nuraghi. In later examples (seventh–sixth centuries)
the walling was sometimes made with greater precision, with
wedge⁄shaped stones recalling the contemporary masonry of
some Giants' Tombs. The wells naturally vary in plan, in   *Fig. 25d*
technique of building and in depth, and in some cases where
the water supply was very meagre a big stone trough formed
the bottom of the reservoir, so that some water remained even
after the water⁄level had fallen. This was the case at Lorana

(Orune). In other instances the stairway may be wedge-shaped in plan, rather than parallel-sided, or it may be placed eccentrically to the well, as for example at Santu Millanu (Nuragus).

A paved area, sometimes protected by walls projecting from the well-structure, is a usual feature, and here are frequently found stone benches for holding the offerings or for seating the participants at the rites. Here too may have been altars for libations, and stone stands for infixing the votive bronzes.

The stone for building the wells and superstructure was not always found in the immediate vicinity, and at Santu Millanu the basalt was transported from over six miles away.

Certain features occur which are also encountered in the Giants' Tombs, but their chronological significance is not yet understood. These features include stone benches in many examples, side-wings forming a sort of forecourt at Su Putzu (Orroli) and at Sa Testa (Olbia) where these are carried round to form a circular enclosure, and the offering niche in the wall above the benches at Su Lamarzu (Rebeccu). The Su Putzu well has been regarded as an early example perhaps dating to the ninth–eighth centuries or so, since its cupola is tall like those of the archaic nuraghi; but at Fontana Coperta, Ballao, where the cupola is also tall, the stones are cut with the greater skill and precision normally attributed to a slightly later date. In fact the development of the well cupola seems to have taken place rather later than that of the nuraghi, and its height may be dictated more by the depth of the water-level than by other considerations.

Plate 40

Dating evidence is not often very satisfactory; most of the nuragic pottery and weapons continued unchanged for too long to be chronologically significant where foreign influences cannot be detected, and the bronze figurines can only be dated stylistically. Moreover, as has been stressed, the waters, particularly those with medicinal qualities, often continued to be

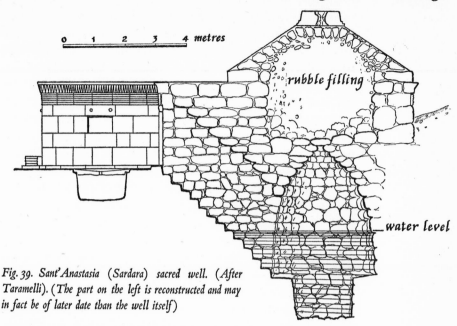

Fig. 39. Sant'Anastasia (Sardara) sacred well. (After Taramelli). (The part on the left is reconstructed and may in fact be of later date than the well itself)

venerated for many centuries. Our main evidence must depend on imported objects which can be dated in their place of origin.

Of the sacred wells which have been excavated, three have especial interest. The earliest, and certainly structurally the most archaic, is in the Campidano at Sardara, near the church of Sant'Anastasia. Its initial date probably falls within the eighth or early seventh century. Here the waters were venerated for their medicinal qualities, and the Christian saint inherited the reputation for healing which had originated about a thousand years earlier.

Fig. 39

Only the lower courses of the cupola were left at the time of the excavation; the walling of the well and the steps were of a rougher finish than in later examples. A big pit containing animal bones and sherds of nuragic pottery was discovered in

Fig. 58

Plate 67

front of the well. The paved area was unusually extensive here, and opening from this (under the present church) was a smaller well filled with a deposit of pottery at the bottom, sealed by a layer containing basalt blocks from the well-head; above this was more pottery, this time with Punic elements. The Nuragic pots and strainers were often decorated with angular incised lines, circles and dots, related perhaps to the painted designs of paleo-Etruscan wares of the late eighth century. The same period is suggested by an oblique-mouthed jug which has two yellow stripes on a dark ground painted round the neck, like Punic examples of the eighth–sixth centuries. Another oblique-mouthed jug had bosses and cordons recalling some from Vetulonia (Poggio della Guardia), and the strainers seem related to those from Finocchito and Pantalica in Sicily. One interesting sherd was decorated in relief just below the rim with a figure holding a forked object resembling some bronzes regarded as ritual, and another sherd is made in the form of a phallus and breasts. A few big bronze 'pins' were associated with this pottery, most of which reflects commercial contacts outside the island, probably initiated by the Phoeni-cians.

The rest of the finds came from the vicinity of the well structure, or from the material between this and its outer revetment. They included large numbers of bronze objects torn from their sockets, a votive quiver, a ship-lamp, and a simple fibula with slightly swollen bow and rhomboid section like archaic examples from Chiusi, etc. Parts of a decorative frieze of chevrons from the well is now in the church. Taramelli has shown this in a hypothetical reconstruction of the façade; but unfortunately he has incorporated elements which may have formed part of a secondary rebuilding, and it cannot therefore be accepted. It is not known to which phase the stylised bull's head carved in stone belonged. This was found near the well, and testifies to the fact that, apart from the water

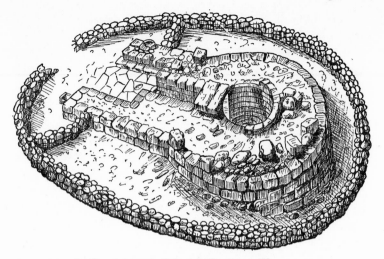

Fig. 40. Sacred well at S. Vittoria di Serri. (After Taramelli)

deity and the fertility god, men still dimly recalled the bull cult which had perhaps survived from the Copper Age when examples carved in low relief were found over tombs at Anghelu Ruju, and from even earlier precursors of these in the East Mediterranean cultures.

At Santa Vittoria (Serri) the big sanctuary excavated by Taramelli, a sacred well occupied the focal point around which other buildings of various dates were grouped. This sacred reservoir had three main elements, the well itself, the stair, and a paved atrium or courtyard in front. The well was carefully made of squared blocks, and was filled not from a vein of water, but by rainwater conducted down a gutter made with stones laid in a V-shape. Holes in the walling were left at intervals to permit drainage. Very little of the cupola remained, only the lower courses, and it may have been dismantled by the Carthaginians so that they could use its stones in another building. In this example the cupola was well above ground, and was evidently covered with a revetted mound.

Fig. 40, Plate 43

133

The outer walling projected to form two parallel-sided wings enclosing an area paved with white limestone, and flanked with benches. In this area, immediately above the steps, was a kind of altar with a hole for poured libations which then flowed through a duct under the paving to a pit below. Stands for fixing ex-voto offerings were found here.

The site afforded no stratification such as might have enabled us to obtain at least a relative date for the many bronzes and other finds made in the vicinity. Various architectural frag-ments, one with a dentellated design perhaps from a cornice and analogous to other fragments from two Giants' Tombs, probably reflect Graeco-Italic influence of the seventh–sixth centuries. A carved stone base or altar similar to one from the well at Mazzani recalls Punic carving and together these details lead us to infer a date of about the sixth century for the well. A large piece of a carved bull's head came from the atrium, again emphasising the persistence of this cult which continued into Roman times, as is attested by the splendid

Plate 77

bronze head of Punico-Roman date from Orani.

Fig. 41

The most beautiful of the excavated wells is at Su Tempiesu (Orune). This is a graceful and sophisticated structure, suffi-ciently well preserved to allow Lilliu to publish a suggested reconstruction. An open ante-room with benches leads to a trapeze-shaped stair (the gaps between its steps were stopped with lead to prevent leakage), and at the foot of the steps is the well itself.

Plate 41

The whole structure was built with obliquely cut stones, basalt or trachite brought from a distance. The masonry is technically advanced, and the building had a pent roof, over-hanging sculptured eaves, as well as an architrave made with curved stones like that of one of the temples at Serra Orrios and recently recognised in some Giants' Tombs as well. On the crest of the roof was a kind of *acroterion* with bronze objects, presumably swords, set with their points upwards, a feature which has no recorded parallels in Sardinia, but recalls Etruscan decoration of the sixth–fifth centuries. Bossed stones in the façade again recall ornamental features not only on Giants' Tombs but on the temple at Serra Orrios and the well at Sant'Anastasia, Sardara.

Some big bronze pins like those from Abini (eighth–seventh centuries) and Forraxi Nioi (seventh century), of a type which lagged on at least into the sixth century, were found to have been stuck horizontally between the stones of the ante-room wall. This temple, excluding certain later additions, seems to belong to the seventh–sixth centuries.

So unusual and sophisticated a sacred well, or well-temple, must owe some inspiration to contacts with the outside world. Greeks from Sicily or Italy probably reached Sardinia by the seventh century or before, and prior to them, Phoenicians and Etruscans; it is possible too that there was a small nucleus of Etruscans living in the north-east of the island. Some building

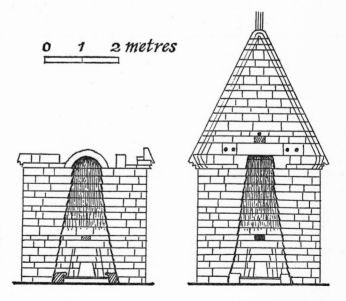

Fig. 41. Section and ideal reconstruction of sacred well at Su Tempiesu (Orune). (After Lilliu)

elements may well have been inspired by these sources. For the pent roof, however, there is a long indigenous ancestry, beginning with the Copper or Bronze Age rock-cut tombs at S. Andrea Priu, and again shown in the bronze model of the small house beside a nuraghe from Ittireddu, in the museum at Cagliari.

From the evidence at our disposal it would seem that none of these sacred wells and springs were built much earlier than about the ninth century. The concept may have been indigenous, but this is improbable, especially as the practice of depositing offerings in wells is found as close by as north Italy (at Panighina, near Bertinoro, for instance) at an earlier date. Moreover, wells of tholos type are also known from Cumae and in Latium. But perhaps it is more probable that for the Sardinian wells inspiration came from another direction, from the Eastern Mediterranean at the time of the trade contacts with the Phoenicians. For at Tell el-Taannack and other Canaanite sites, somewhat similar wells, reached by a flight of steps, are known, though they may be earlier by several centuries. Once introduced, the cult continued to develop in its local form among the indigenous peoples, and its associated architecture was adapted to the constructional repertoire already established in the nuraghi and the Giants' Tombs. The majority were made between the ninth–sixth centuries, it seems; some were then sacked by the Carthaginians, and others remained untouched, to be venerated for many centuries. In the areas not affected by Carthaginian penetration, sacred wells may have been constructed in the subsequent centuries.

TEMPLES

Evidently most of the religious life in the Nuragic period was centred first around the Giants' Tombs, and slightly later on at the sacred wells and sanctuaries. But three temples are

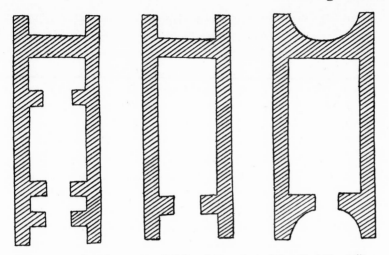

Fig. 42. Plans of temples at Esterzili (left) and Serra Orrios (Dorgali). (After Lilliu and Ceruti) (Not to scale)

known which do not seem to owe their architectural style wholly to local inspiration, and outside influences from the Greek world are suspected.

Two of these temples are at Serra Orrios, in the village near Dorgali already described, and the third is the so-called Domus de Orgia at Cuccureddi, near Esterzili. Although the plan of all three is basically similar, each has its own characteristics. The larger of the two buildings at Serra Orrios is enclosed within an irregular stone-walled *temenos*. The presence of a decorative or symbolic boss or breast on the left wall of the entrance, the curved stone lintels over the entrance and the curved forecourt and benches all link it stylistically with the sacred wells and Giants' Tombs; the plan, however, seems to be foreign. The other, smaller, temple stands in a spacious circular *temenos*, and is orientated towards the south-east rather than to the full south as are the other two examples. In plan it is more angular. Both buildings were made with coursed

Fig. 42, Plate 41

blocks, and probably had a pent roof. On the strength of the architectural analogies with the Giants' Tombs and the well-temples or sacred wells at Santa Vittoria (Serri) and Su Tempiesu (Orune), it is thought that the Serra Orrios temples may date from the seventh–sixth centuries.

Perhaps a little later in date is the building at Esterzili, examined by Contu and dated hypothetically to the sixth century or later. It was built with schist blocks in regular courses, and around it was an oval *temenos* delimiting the sacred area. It is a double *in antis* plan resembling the megaron of Greek tradition, and is somewhat larger than the other two, measuring a little less than 20 metres over-all. But in this temple the wall slopes slightly inwards, particularly on the inside, and it is possible that it had a false cupola roofing like some of the nuragic passages, or even that it had a rounded covering like some of the Giants' Tombs.

The plan of these three temples is unlikely to be an entirely indigenous conception, though rectangular buildings are known from early contexts at Monte d'Accoddi and elsewhere. It is more probable that, like the sacred well of Su Tempiesu, some foreign architectural style influenced their construction. Lilliu has suggested Graeco-Siciliot ideas introduced by Phoenicio-Punic settlers, and certainly these people must have been accustomed to seeing archaic Greek temples in Sicily. Contu has emphasised the distance of our two sites from centres of Greek or Punic influence, but the truth is that we have only a very vague picture of Greek activities in Sardinia. It is possible that Olbia was a short-lived Greek colony founded by Iolaus with Thespians and Athenians, for Diodorus Siculus writes of these Greeks withdrawing from the plains into the mountains and there mixing with the indigenous peoples. Certainly the name Olbia is a Greek one, and it must be remembered that by 560 BC Corsica had a Phocaean colony, and the same people could have been established for a short time in north-east Sardinia. But there is some confusion in Diodorus's account, for he places the Corsican colony at Kalaris, and no such town exists. Perhaps, as Dunbabin suggests, he mis-spelt, and misplaced, the Sardinian town of Karalis.

Siciliot mercenaries were probably conscripted into the Carthaginian army, and by the sixth century a pact of friendship between Sybarites and Sardinians attests trading relations in the Tyrrhenian seaways.

At all events it was perfectly possible in one way or another for the local masons to have been attracted to copy Greek architectural plans, about which they may have heard at second hand. The small temples we have described may have been the result.

It has not yet been possible to identify the 'Temple of Sardus Pater', which Ptolemy mentions on the west coast of the island; nor can we guess what type of temple it was. The traditional site of this temple was at Capo della Frasca, near Narrubiu, by the Bay of Oristano.

VILLAGES, CITADELS AND SANCTUARIES

We have seen that in pre-nuragic times the Copper and Bronze Age villages such as San Gemiliano (Sestu) consisted of groups of huts perhaps inhabited by only a few families, driven to live together for collective security against the dangers and difficulties of their natural habitat. Gradually, however, with the clearing of woods and the opening up of more pasture-land, and with the hazards of their environment partially overcome as a result of evolving techniques and increased experience, it was possible for small groups of people to leave the villages and to farm individually. By the time of the earlier nuraghi, the settlement pattern seems to have broken down into smaller units. A few hundred years later, in the first half of the first millennium B C or even before, there was once again need for collective security.

The tribal system was crystallising, based perhaps less on ethnic groups than on the federal and military alliances which, particularly under the threat of invasion, bound the smaller communities into bigger complexes. With the rapidly evolving civilisation brought to a climax by the exploitation of copper and other mineral resources for what was then becoming an international market, the political organisation was hastened into being. The small coastal markets were developed by the Phoenicians into larger urban colonies having trade rela-tions with the native Sardinians, who were galvanised into taking collective political and commercial action in order to profit by the situation to their best advantage. We must also remember that greater specialisation is a corollary of an advancing civilisation. Men practising individual crafts are in increasing demand in the villages: leather and metal-workers, miners, hunters, warriors, shepherds, weavers, masons, priests and so on, for it was no longer possible for each man to cater for his own needs. So we find the develop-ment of larger and larger villages, looking for protection either to a redesigned and refortified nuraghe such as Su Nuraxi (Barumini), or sometimes to a row of nuraghi placed at strategic points of vantage, as at Serrucci. No doubt, too, isolated nuraghi continued to be built in parts of the island where the local conditions favoured their use.

Few of the large concentrations of huts are likely to have been fully established before the Phoenician settlement, and it is from the sixth century onwards that the historical sources emphasise the dual character of the Sardinian population; the nuragic culture of the south and west, strongly influenced by the new Punico-Sardinian culture centred around the urban, coastal settlements on the one hand, and on the other the isolated mountain tribes cut off from outside contacts except perhaps from Corsica and Etruria, and living in a tired and decaying state of civilisation. It was now that the upland sanctuaries reached their full importance in the social and religious life of the people.

The nuragic overlords had probably by now lost their power, and had given place to oligarchies of nobles and priests. In fact the characteristics of the sanctuaries, with their council-chambers, their sacred well and sometimes also a foundry, emphasise the growing importance of the priests and the metalworkers engaged in producing the innumerable votive statuettes and other objects offered to the gods at the sacred sites.

Such a social pattern endured, in some isolated areas outside the effective range of Carthaginian interference, into the Imperial Roman period and even later. To this day many aspects of Sardinian life, in the Barbagia particularly, still reflect those of the late nuragic period. These aspects include not only the social ones such as vendettas, cattle-thieving and so on, but also clothing, for the black stocking caps worn by the men are closely paralleled in some of the nuragic bronze statuettes, while the oxen whose horns are decorated on feast days with pierced oranges also find their counterpart among the bronzes. Nor must one forget that some of the remote sanctuaries, far from the villages, are still sometimes used for village meetings.

About 100 nuragic villages are known to exist all over Sardinia, and we have a chronological guide to the develop-ment of one from the excavations at Barumini, whose story has, probably, a far wider than purely local significance.

In the earliest village at Barumini a small group of huts near the nuraghe date from the first half of the eighth century B C, and include rectangular houses as well as oval ones. Both types are built in a tradition which had already lasted some centuries in Sardinia. The masonry was simple and consisted

Fig. 34

of small stones mixed with clay 'mortar'. One of the rectangular huts was paved and had a number of round holes in the
floor, which is thought to have been for votive deposits: in
them were pots containing ashes and the remains of birds and
small animals.

Lilliu estimates that by the time the village was greatly
enlarged between the mid eighth and the late sixth century,
some 200–300 people could have been living around the
nuraghe, perhaps mostly troops, but also, no doubt, various
craftsmen. The huts, about 60 of them so far excavated, were
by now almost always circular, built with stone blocks and
roofed with branches and stone slabs, or thatched, like the
present-day shepherds' *pinnettas* whose conical roofs are such a
characteristic feature of the Sardinian scene. These huts were
arranged in groups round a central open space or piazza. One
particularly large building belongs to this phase. Circular
like the others, it has a stone bench around the inside, and
above this are recesses for holding lamps or, maybe, objects of
religious significance; for inside this hut (perhaps a council
chamber where the elders and priests discussed village matters)
was found a sacred baetyl representing a nuraghe, as well as a
stone trough and various objects of stone, pottery and metal.
The village also produced querns, ovens, votive statuettes, etc.
It came to a violent end, after being besieged and dismantled
by the Carthaginians.

The next village, represented by about 20 houses, was built
on the remains of the old one by people returning to live there
again, early in the fifth century BC. By now some of the
houses are more sophisticated; they have a single entrance
leading into a central courtyard from which radiate a number
of other rooms, each apparently with its own function:
living room, sleeping room, kitchen, bread-making room, and
so on. Buildings similar in type to these were found in earlier
contexts at both Serra Orrios (Dorgali) and Santa Vittoria

(Serri). Stone basins for kneading dough were found in some of them. A large number of objects in bronze, iron, terracotta and vitreous paste, as well as the pottery, point to a traditional way of life, though decadent and impoverished.

The last phase of the village belongs to the Punico-Roman period (third–first centuries B C), and the finds included a number of imported objects, Etruscan-Campanian pottery, small bronze bells and Carthaginian and Roman coins, hinting not only at trade, but also perhaps at racial inter-marriage.

At Serra Orrios, near Dorgali, another large village was excavated in 1936–37; extensive areas of it were found intact, including streets, small piazzas with communal wells, two temples and a large number of huts. This village dates from before the end of the sixth century, and is again close to a nuraghe to which its inhabitants may have looked for protection, though in this case, being well to the east of the main area of Punic penetration, it may have enjoyed a long and relatively peaceful life. Plate 42, *Fig. 43*

Not far to the east of Serra Orrios, at a site near Cala Gonone, is another big concentration of huts clustered round the nuraghe called Arvu. Here are over 114 huts, all round or oval except for one rectangular one which produced only Roman pottery, not the nuragic ware found in the other excavated huts. This village is thought to be a very late one. It had no defensive wall and was probably sacked by the Romans. This seems to suggest that simple types of nuraghe continued to be built until very late in the pre-Roman period.

Another big village of more than 100 huts can be found at Serrucci (Gonnesa) in the south-west near Porto Paglia. It was associated with two Giants' Tombs and a nuraghe, and was provided with its own water reservoir. Some of the huts were sophisticated, and had windows with jambs and lintel, but this is not surprising as the site was occupied down into

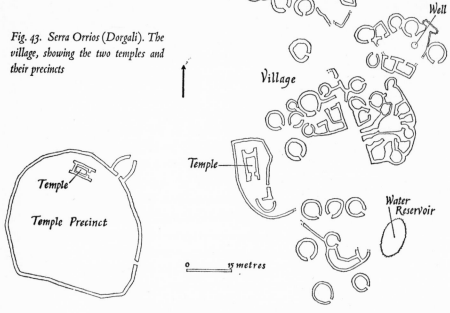

Fig. 43. Serra Orrios (Dorgali). The village, showing the two temples and their precincts

Roman times. Protected by a triple line of nuraghi guarding the coast, it may have been the political centre for most of the Sulcis (southern Iglesiente).

The citadels in the upland areas were far more effectively defended, often being built in wild, rocky and wooded country. By no means all of them have been charted, and more probably still remain to be discovered. Some have only been visited by shepherds and woodmen. Their characteristic feature is a strong containing wall, sometimes punctuated with towers, inside which stood a cluster of huts. The inhabitants must have had to live largely by hunting, and some of the citadels may only have been occupied intermittently, when danger drove the inhabitants of the near-by villages and nuraghi to seek the greater safety of an inaccessible and well hidden fortress.

One citadel at Saurecci (Guspini) occupies a high peak overlooking the Campidano. The massive walls are built with three incorporated towers, an unusual plan which recalls the talayotic village at Les Salines in Majorca. Another defended village is at Su Chiai (Lanusei).

Perhaps the strangest of all the mountain retreats is at Monte Tiscali, reached from Dorgali. Here on a rocky peak is an immense karstic cave, now open to the sky in the middle; presumably the roof fell in in ancient times, as the huts built inside the cave are placed on each side of the fallen rocks. The walls of these huts, of which there are both round and rectangular ones, are unusually thin; even so, many of them still stand to a considerable height, making the huts look like little towers. Excavations have revealed that this village was occupied in the Roman period, and indeed when the classical writers referred to the Sardinians as living in caves in Punic times, they may have had in mind just such places as Monte Tiscali and the gallery nuraghi. According to Diodorus Siculus and Strabo, it was only possible for the Carthaginians to take Sardinians prisoner when they temporarily left their hide-outs to go to public feasts and assemblies.

Yet another type of stronghold is at Sa Sea (Tresnuraghes) where the extreme south-west point of an upland plateau is cut across by a huge wall 4 metres wide. This makes, in effect, a kind of promontory fort and resembles others in the central uplands of the island. They are not yet datable.

Many strongholds had a special significance in the religious life of the people, and can be regarded as sanctuaries. Here sacrifices and votive bronze objects were offered to the gods, and here too the *festas* and assemblies for all the district around took place. At Cabu Abbas, high on a hill above Olbia, a huge megalithic wall, standing in places over 5 metres in height and pierced by two lintelled doorways, encloses a Nuragic building containing a well found to be full of burnt bones and potsherds. (But this appears to be an unusually strongly defended nuraghe rather than a sanctuary, as supposed by Taramelli.) Another at Orulu, near Orgosolo, consisted of a Nuragic village above which a rock-cut stair led up to a rough altar. A big votive deposit from this village included weapons, ship-lamps, etc.; the Punic and Roman coins also found suggest that the sanctity of the site lasted long. It may have been, like Monte su Ballu, one of the strong places dominating the biggest of all the sanctuaries, that of Abini (Teti) right in the heart of Sardinia. First reported by Fiorelli in 1878, this site, in a rocky and lonely countryside, has never been systematically excavated; instead, it has been looted and pillaged by treasure-seekers. The site itself occupies a hollow with steep mountains on all sides but one, from which a small rivulet flows out towards the Tirso valley. In the early accounts some sort of a stone enclosure was reported to have contained a large jar near to various groups of bronzes; around this structure were many hut foundations. Subsequently a plan was drawn showing a large nuraghe with four angle towers, but Taramelli, who carried out checking excavations a few years later, failed to identify this, finding instead an interesting stone building with an internal bench round the wall. Opening off this was a spring, once covered with a cupola, whose water flowed into a stone trough and thence to a pit or well in the long elliptical enclosure annexed to the main building. The entire structure was made of big granite blocks. Here in one building are united the three elements generally found separately in other sanctuaries: the big enclosure, the council chamber and the sacred well. The fourth element sometimes present, a foundry, was not discovered, but enormous quantities of bronzes, many of which were dispersed, hint that one was probably not far away. The bronzes recovered from this site, possibly the principal sanctuary of the Iliensi, are described on page 169. They belong to the seventh–sixth centuries B C.

Another sanctuary, more fully excavated but again without modern stratigraphical observation, was found at Santa Vittoria, a high, flat-topped basalt *giara* or plateau above the village of Gergei, some miles to the east of Barumini. This sanctuary seems originally to have developed round a nuraghe which was later dismantled and its stones re-used. The small medieval church of Santa Vittoria probably marks its site. The complex, which at one phase was weakly defended by a wall, was continually undergoing alterations and new build-ings were erected over a long period of years. One of the earliest and most remarkable of these was the sacred well described on p. 133, which belongs to the eighth–seventh centuries. It was probably this building which formed the focal point of the sanctuary.

Another pre-Punic structure was the *Recinto Ipetrale*, or open enclosure, as it was called by Taramelli who was con-vinced that it could never have been roofed owing to its large internal diameter (11 metres). This was a circular construction with a single entrance, its walls sloping slightly inwards. An internal ledge or cornice about 1 metre in width ran right round the interior of the enclosure. Whether this was simply to protect those sitting on the bench below, or whether it was intended to support the wooden floor of a loft above, it is difficult to decide. Perhaps the latter is more probable, as the wall carries on up beyond the cornice, and a parallel for the ledge, though smaller, exists at the nuraghe Oes near Sant' Antine at Torralba. Close to the wall inside was found a limestone altar and an offering trough; another big basin, perhaps for ritualistic ablutions, was near the entrance. In many respects this building resembles the one at Forraxi Nioi in which the seventh-century hoard of bronzes was dis-covered. On the cobbled floor lay a thick deposit of animal and other remains, carbonised material and ashes, suggesting that sacrifices had been made here. The finds included many bronze animal figurines representing bull, cow, boar and goat, and also sheet metal, a ship-lamp, a small dagger of Forraxi Nioi and Abini type, and much pottery of Nuragic type as well as Punic sherds and a Phoenicio-Cypriot candelabrum of the seventh–sixth centuries, very similar to another from San Vero Milis. The building lasted, therefore, into the late sixth century or even later.

Another pre-Punic building (later incorporated in a big porticoed assembly enclosure) was called the Double-axe enclosure after the discovery of a bronze double-axe perhaps once worshipped here, and thought to have been set in the stone base also recovered. This structure was round and measured less than 7 metres in diameter. The lower courses of its walls were made with basalt blocks, and the upper, marking a rebuilding, with an admixture of white limestone; the floor paving too had been relaid at a higher level. The original floor was covered with a deposit of purely nuragic character, and this was sealed by a secondary paving on which lay a thick layer of ashes, animal bones, nuragic and Punic pottery, and beads. The chronological sequence seems to have been as follows: the building was erected before the late sixth century and evidently contained a baetyl or altar. It was des-troyed by the Carthaginians and then re-designed. The walls were raised, the floor was re-paved, and the old altar replaced with a taller one, topped, perhaps, by the double-axe. This building seems to have been roofed with wedge-shaped stones taken from the cupola of the destroyed sacred well.

The big porticoed enclosure was evidently designed to incorporate this and other earlier elements, and was built much later, perhaps even in Roman times. Its outer wall was found standing to a height of nearly 2 metres, and was made of trachite blocks arranged in courses with clay 'mortar'. The portico was evidently roofed with rafters resting on the outer wall and on internal pilasters, and covered with stone slabs. The occupation material consisted of Nuragic pottery from the lower levels, mixed with Punic and Roman ware above.

A group of buildings to the east of this also appears to have been early, as its finds showed no admixture of Punic or Roman elements. The complex either represents a courtyard house with rooms radiating from a court like some from the early fifth-century phase at Barumini, or was a group of small huts clustered round a little square. One of these rooms contained a curious double stone baetyl, dotted with little holes on its upper surface, intended for holding the lead fixtures of votive offerings.

Many other buildings have been excavated and described, including a large rectangular construction containing many votive objects, pottery, altars, and so forth. It is thought to have been a temple, but the masonry denotes more than one building phase, and the very complex nature of the site makes it impossible, without more advanced methods of excavation and section drawing, to clarify the purpose or sequence of the buildings.

One of the many unusual sites which still remains to be excavated is at Luvunneri (Bitti). Here a huge wall of big granite blocks encloses an area measuring about 30 metres across. It has an interior bench, and a kind of altar stands in the centre. Whether this forms part of another sanctuary can only be ascertained by excavation.

At Golgo (Baunei) a cult centre, not yet well explored as it is high up in the mountains, produced a quantity of votive bronzes including among other things statuettes, swords and a ship-lamp. Another sanctuary was found accidentally at Olmedo in the Nurra. The citadel still remains but its sacred well was destroyed by treasure-seekers, though fortunately the votive deposit remained intact. This included a bronze model of a nuraghe, a statuette with hands raised in prayer and several

Plate 33

149

figures of animals, including mouflons and oxen (*Bos sardo*, which still exist in some parts of the Ogliastra). Copper cakes, or bun ingots, were also recovered, as well as spearheads with lead soldering for attaching them to a stone base.

As we have stressed, these sanctuaries lasted into the Roman period. The well known bronze base of a votive column, in, scribed in Greek, Punic and Latin from San Nicolò at Gerrei, dedicated to Merres, Aesculapius and Esmun by one of the slaves of the salt,workers, was found in a sanctuary associated with a therapeutic well. This column probably belonged to the early second century B C.

Plate 76

CHAPTER V

The Nuragic Culture:
Metalworking and Pottery

MINING, SMELTING AND CASTING

IN THE EARLIER PART of the Nuragic period, some copper at least was being imported from the East Mediterranean, as we have seen from the ingots found at Assemini and near the nuraghi at Serra Ilixi and Ozieri discussed on page 110. But as time went on more and more nuraghi seem to have had an associated foundry where the weapons and implements in everyday use were cast, probably from locally found metal. And we have already seen that in the sanctuaries and near the sacred wells the foundries played an essential part in the production of votive objects.

The Phoenicians had learnt the techniques of metal-mining from the Egyptians, and even if in Sardinia the exploitation of local ores may have begun in pre-Phoenician times, we can reasonably expect a considerable acceleration in metallurgy after their arrival. By the Full Nuragic period the huge quantities of bronzes, moulds made of local stone, copper cakes and rejects from casting point to a very well developed industry; nor is evidence lacking for the mining methods used.

We know that the Iglesiente was, and still is, richer in mineral ores than any other part of Sardinia. Here in Nuragic times silver seems to have been mined, perhaps first by the Phoenicians, for according to Diodorus Siculus they acquired increased power through their trade in silver extracted from Spain and Sardinia. By Roman times silver may have been mined in the Ballao district, in the south-east. Lead too was

mined in the Iglesiente, and in all probability the small cos-
metic jars and other objects found in the Carthaginian tombs
were of locally mined lead, for Carthaginian objects have been
recovered from some of the open mining shafts. But before
this, lead was used for fixing votive objects in their stands and
for filling the interstices in the stonework of certain monuments. Near Guspini, lead dross has been found associated
with nuragic type mace-heads, and pots mended with lead
come from the nuraghi of Palmavera, Losa, Lugherras, etc.
The lead mines near Rosas and Narcao in the Iglesiente have
also produced mace-heads of Nuragic (but not precisely
datable) type from the vicinity.

One of the regions most carefully studied for its vestiges of
mining is in the Barbagia, surrounding the upper reaches of
the Flumendosa river. Here, near Gadoni, Aritzo and Laconi,
a wild and desolate region has been completely denuded of its
natural forest by copper miners who have left not only their
quarries for superficial mining, but also some galleries following metalliferous veins, as well as actual shafts, sometimes sunk
to a depth of as much as 70 feet. At the bottom of one of these
the skeleton of a miner crushed by a fallen boulder was found
beside the material he had selected for smelting.

The methods used were primitive. The mineral was pounded
into small fragments with heavy pounders and pestles, and
then taken away to be smelted, evidently at no great distance
from the mining areas. No iron objects or signs of Punic or
Roman occupation have been observed in this important
district, and as Taramelli has emphasised, 'the enormous
industry of mining, searching for metals, digging and dis-
burdening reflects native, not Carthaginian or Phoenician
work.' The metal for the bronzes from the near-by Abini and
Forraxi Nioi hoards probably came from these mines; which
could well have been in production in approximately the
eighth-fifth centuries B C or later.

In the same locality, near Fontana Raminosa, large quantities of mineral ores ready for smelting were found together with slag and the remains of very thick-sided pots or crucibles showing signs of intense heat inside. Copper was the chief product of these mines, but silver also may have been extracted. Again, at Nuraghe Nieddiu, several of the huts nearby produced nuragic pottery, a number of copper bun-ingots, flat and lenticular in shape, as well as troughs made from basalt brought from a distance as the local limestone would not have served the purpose.

Nearer to the Campidano, at Barrali on its eastern borders, were found some huge, almost cylindrical pestles made of diorite, rounded and much worn at the ends and weighing about 18 lb. each. These presumably served for pounding the mineral ores. Near-by were other stone implements including mace-heads, often associated with mining.

The source of the tin, found for example as cassiterite in the Forraxi Nioi hoard and elsewhere, is not yet known with certainty; but according to recent analyses the cassiterite from nuragic sites was imported, perhaps from Spain or southern France. That located in Sardinia in recent years does not seem to have been exploited, nor is it known when the Tuscany tin was first used.

The actual smelting was carried out in most cases near either a nuraghe or a nuragic sanctuary, and a fortunate discovery at Ortu Commidu (Sardara) has given valuable information concerning the methods used. On a little rise not far from Sardara and its sacred well of Sant'Anastasia, is a nuraghe to which, in a secondary phase before the sixth century BC four subsidiary towers were added. The lower courses of two of these remained when the site was excavated by Taramelli, who found that they had been re-used as a foundry for smelting copper in about the fourth–third centuries. A huge earthenware ring nearly 1 metre in diameter was found in one of these.

Fig. 44

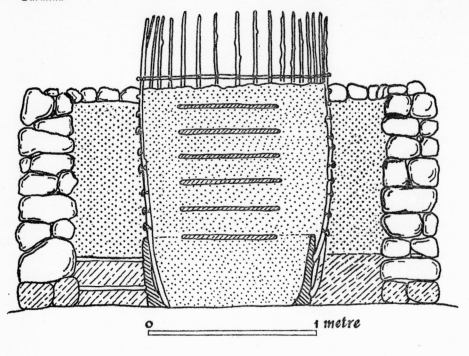

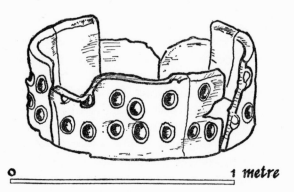

Fig. 44. Metal foundry at Ortu Commidu (Sardara). (After Taramelli). Above, the terracotta receptacle is shown in section with alternative reconstructions to left and right

The outer surface of this trough-like container had been studded with round hollows, thought to serve for holding the
framework of a cage or basket-like contrivance which would
have been filled with alternate layers of mineral ores and
charcoal. Between this and the surrounding walls combustible
material was packed, and ignited from below through a
draught hole. Additional layers of mineral ores and charcoal
could be added from time to time; the metal then dropped
down into the earthenware container, where it hardened into
lumps and copper cakes. Other small associated enclosures
contained stone crucibles and evidence of intense heat. Black
ware, characteristic of the fourth-century Punic tombs at
Tharros and Nora, was recovered from the upper levels on the
site and the foundry must belong to that date or not much
later. Thought by Taramelli to have represented a complex
designed *ab initio* as a foundry in the Nuragic period, Lilliu
has subsequently drawn attention to its three phases: the simple
tower dating from about the eighth century, its re-fortification
in about the sixth, and finally a foundry built in the ruins in
the fourth–third centuries B C.

Other evidence of skilled metallurgy comes from the
numerous stone moulds from all over the island. Examples
have been found for casting many types of weapons including
flat and socketed axes, double-axes, spearheads (some with an
octagonal socket), triangular daggers of Abini type, sickles,
etc. These moulds are made of schist, greenstone or steatite,
and not infrequently both the upper and lower surfaces of the
stone were used. Founder's rejects are occasionally discovered
too. A large mould from Urzulei was found in a cave with
a group of bronze statuettes, but these must have been made
with the more complicated method of *cire-perdue*.

As we have seen, both the Carthaginians and the Romans
continued to exploit the mineral resources of the island. The
Romans, in fact, founded two mining settlements: one in the

island of S. Antioco (the Phoenician *Sulcis*) called *Plumbea*, and the other near the Flumendosa, known as *Metalla*.

WEAPONS, IMPLEMENTS AND HOARDS

The bronze implements belonging to the Nuragic culture in its earlier stages appear to have largely comprised traditional types handed down from the pre-nuragic cultures of the Bronze Age. Indeed, during the five hundred years or so before the dawn of the first millennium, there are very few hints of outside influences in the repertoire; it is only in the Full Nuragic period of the eighth–sixth centuries that these become more frequent. Then foreign implements sometimes served as models to be copied by the local craftsmen, though many other weapons are purely Sardinian in type and seem to have remained unaltered for many years once a satisfactory form had been designed. A certain conservatism in the weapons is, however, offset by the highly varied and individual little bronze statuettes made in large numbers for votive offerings at this time; these are a unique achievement of which Sardinia is rightly proud.

The rich local resources of bronze, the natural conservatism of the people and the Punic occupation which cut off the island from extensive outside contacts combined to preserve a Bronze Age which lingered into the Roman period without any Iron Age transition. From soon after the Punic settle-ment in the sixth century, the island culture began to show signs of tiredness from which it never recovered, and it was quickly surpassed by the Etruscan or Greek-inspired Iron Age cultures of the Italian peninsula and by other cultures in western Europe.

Plate 31 The huge copper ingots from Serra Ilixi, Assemini and Bisarcio (Ozieri) were evidently imported from the eastern Mediterranean in about 1200 BC. The earliest of the double-axes (perhaps endowed with some religious significance) may have arrived at about the same time. Who brought them we do not know, but it is not impossible that they were introduced by returning Shardana. At all events they were destined to be copied in increasing numbers early in the first millennium, when they may have had an exchange value as well as a practical one. The same may be true for the flanged axes of various sizes, often too large or too small for practical use. Birocchi, who made a study of the Sardinian hoards, suggested that those consisting only of flanged or double-axes may ante-date the Full Nuragic period to which most of the bronzes belong. How early they may have been imported we cannot yet say; but evidence is not lacking to show that many were cast in Sardinia, as in the Chilivani hoard and elsewhere the axes had not been refined after casting. These flanged axes are very common and are generally characterised by a straight cutting edge, though occasionally curved blades are found.

Various other types of axe are known by the eighth–sixth centuries when the local metal resources were reaching full development. A few axes with wings and stop ridge may have come in from the Italian mainland or the Rhône valley; there are no moulds for these in Sardinia, so they were probably not locally cast. Looped and flanged axes and double-looped palstaves were imported from Iberia and are present at Forraxi Nioi and Monte Sa Idda. Single-looped palstaves too came from Iberia, where they are sometimes found in association with carp's-tongue swords. Other Iberian types were some of the flat axes with side projections (though these originated earlier in the Near East and could have been brought by Mycenaean traders), and double-looped socket axes, both of which were found at Monte Sa Idda, and the latter type was evidently copied locally, as some are found in an unfinished state. A rare type of axe has a simple form of socket closed with rivets.

Fig. 45

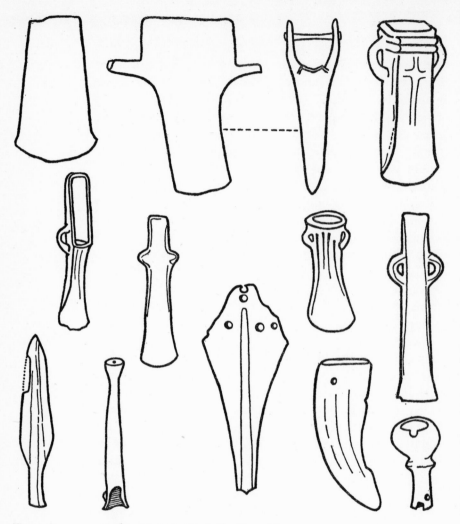

Fig. 45. Bronze weapons from Monte Sa Idda. (After Taramelli)

Spearheads are often exaggeratedly large (one was 43 cm. in length), and the Chilivani type, which was widespread in Sardinia, had a socket which was rounded inside but octag-onal outside. Moulds for these show that they were produced

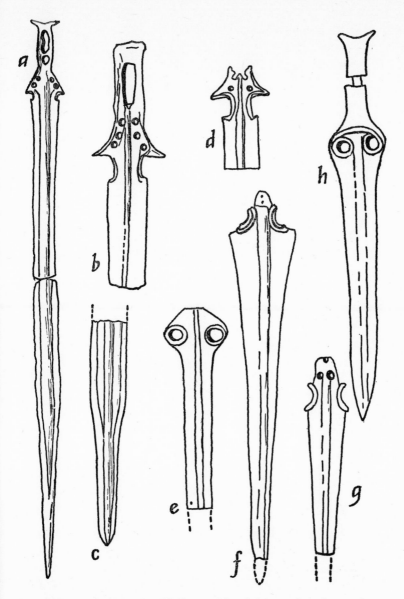

Fig. 46. Weapons from Monte Sa Idda (b, c, e and g) with foreign analogies from Huelva, Spain (a); Populonia (d); Villalba, Spain (f); Asturias, Spain (h)

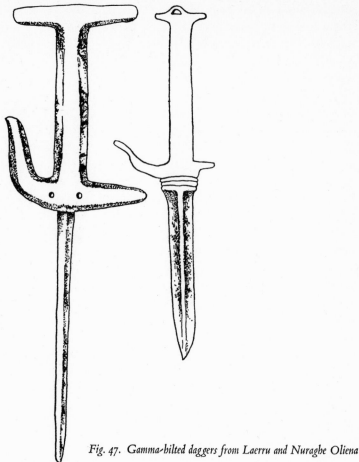

Fig. 47. Gamma-hilted daggers from Laerru and Nuraghe Oliena

locally. Ferrules have the same octagonal section. A mould
from Nuraghe Piscu (Suelli) shows that they too were local
products, and they were present at Abini and Forraxi Nioi.

Daggers of a simple flat type had continued to be used since
pre-nuragic times, but a new and characteristic form with the
so-called *gamma* hilt was evolved in the first millennium and is

Fig. 47

widely found in all parts of the island; it is also to be seen frequently worn by some of the men portrayed in the bronze statuettes. It appears, too, on one side of the little 'votive quivers', and was also probably represented in the punctated design on the curious bronze candelabrum from S. Maria di Tergu. These daggers evidently had either a leather or a bronze sheath; the former is implied by the stylised stitching sometimes shown as a herring-bone design, while an example of a bronze sheath is known from Forraxi Nioi. The hilts vary, and may be in openwork. These daggers were sometimes used as trade objects even as late as the third or second century B C, for one was found with a Punic coin hoard at Aritzo in the Barbagia.

Fig. 55

The votive quivers belong to about the eighth–seventh centuries, as examples came from Phoenicio–Punic contexts at Tharros and Nora, while others came from the hoard of Falda della Guardiola in Populonia, dated to the early seventh century. These quivers often show among their contents some of the big bronze pins or darts (their use is uncertain) so common in Sardinia, and again present in the Punic tombs at Tharros and Nora. Others were found stuck into the walling of the well-temple at Su Tempiesu. Real quivers, which, in proportion to the figure must have been about 65 cm. long, are worn on the back of some of the figurines. They sometimes contain the tall flag-like insignia carried vertically over the left shoulder.

Fig. 54

Sickles are socketed by the time we arrive at the period to which the Abini hoard belongs, but a typologically earlier form came from Samugheo (Fordongianus). Chisels vary greatly in length and may be hexagonal or square in section. Saws, files, drills, mattocks and other implements are also known.

Swords of several varieties and sizes include the immensely long votive swords, sometimes as much as 130 cm. in length,

Plates 44, 45

made for fixing in a stand, and with the tip sometimes piercing a decorative group of figures of men or deer. Of more practical use are the shorter, wider swords, some with midrib, sometimes shown on the statuettes. The well known hoard from Monte Sa Idda produced carp's-tongue swords perhaps imported or inspired from Spain. Their very exaggerated *ricasso* and long pointed shoulders have led Hencken to suggest that they are more evolved than those in the Huelva hoard which has been dated by Hawkes to 700–650.

Figs. 46, 51

Shields can be seen on many of the figurines. Usually round with a central boss and radiating design, they were slung on the back when not in use. Small leather shields are reported by Strabo. Bows and arrows are very common, and many of the tribal chieftains are shown carrying a staff or knobbed stick.

Razors are very rare and were probably imported. A Villa-novan rectangular type with ring handle was found in a nuraghe in the Nurra, and other possible examples exist. Founder's hammers, perhaps used for finishing bronzes after casting, have been included in the hoards at Lotzorai and Lei (Sa Maddalena) and one of unknown provenance is in the Spano collection.

Fig. 48

By the time of the Phoenician settlements in the early eighth century or a little before, it is possible that the local currency had already changed from the primitive ox-unit to the copper ingots, and from these to various sizes of bronze axes. These (according to Birocchi) were soon to give place to copper ingots of a different type, usually plano-convex in shape, and subsequently to *aes signatum* and *aes grave*. The absence of these two latter currencies in Sardinia is due, he suggests, to the Carthaginian occupation which caused the more abrupt change from copper units to coinage at least in the affected areas.

Birocchi has noted that several hoards in Sardinia, and many elsewhere, are exclusively composed of axes; these he would

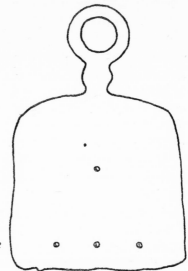

Fig. 48. Razor from a nuraghe in the Nurra

place earlier than the other hoards but later than the Serra Ilixi ingots, namely, at about the beginning of the first millennium. Four hoards may belong to this phase: Sassu, Nule, Oliena and Nuchis. Shortly after these he would place the hoard of Monte Arrubbiu (Sarrok), containing axes associated with copper cakes or ingots. Later again may be the hoards with only copper ingots, at Porto Torres II, Ossi, and two from Olbia (or Terranova as it was previously called) at the nuraghi Chidonza and Criscula. Then come the big classic hoards of the eighth–fifth centuries, such as Chilivani, Abini, Forraxi Nioi and Monte Sa Idda. Apart from the hoards which can be dated by foreign imports, the relative dates of the other groups are purely hypothetical.

Before describing the more important hoards it should be pointed out that only a few may have represented currency deposits; the majority are either votive deposits belonging to a sacred site such as a sanctuary or well-shrine, where votive offerings were made to the gods or to ancestors, or founders' hoards consisting of various objects collected by a founder for re-casting. Both the votive and the founders' hoards may contain bronzes of different dates. It is not always possible to be sure what type of hoard is represented, especially since some of the so-called currency hoards may be nothing more than the stock in trade of a specialised metalworker, and some of the founders' hoards may have consisted of bronzes robbed from sacked or abandoned sacred sites.

We shall now briefly describe some of the principal hoards, limiting ourselves to the more significant among the fifty or so known.

Nule (Currency hoard, ninth–eighth centuries?)

Accidentally discovered in a nuragic village near Nuraghe Sisine. The hoard had been buried under a granite slab, and comprised 21 big flanged axes with thickened centres and curved blades. This is a common type in Sardinia and the axes may have been used for tree-felling if not for currency. The examples from Nule were all of the same form but varied in size.

Monte Arrubbiu (*Sarrok*) (Founder's hoard, eighth–seventh centuries?)

Found in a pottery jar buried in a hillside near Sarrok. The contents were: 1 large flat axe with two loops (length 22.5 cm.); 2 double-looped palstaves (length 21 cm.); 1 hoe (length 15 cm.); 7 rough castings of hatchets of a type similar to those from Modica in Sicily (about ninth century) but more robust; a number of metal cakes and about 23 lb. weight of broken metal. This hoard must be dated by the looped axes which were presumably imported from Iberia, and may be contemporaneous with, or not much earlier than, the Monte Sa Idda hoard.

Chilivani (*Ozieri*) (Founder's hoard, eighth–seventh centuries?)

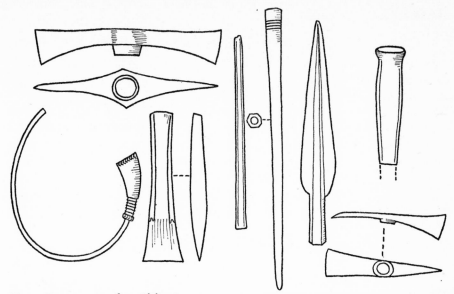

Fig. 49. Bronze weapons from Chilivani

Fig. 49

Found in a big earthenware jar which was broken, many of
the bronzes being dispersed. The pot, which was about 60 cm.
tall and with a heavy flat rim of a kind known from Nuragic
sites, contained about 80 whole or broken bronzes. Amongst
these were: 8 double-axes with vertical blades and one with a
mattock blade; 1 double-axe ingot 39 cm. long; 49 flanged
axes with straight blades and varying in length from 17–21
cm.; 10 spearheads with octagonal socket, from 27–43 cm. in
length; 3 ferrules; 5 chisels with square or hexagonal section
and up to 32 cm. long; 1 cone-shaped ornament of unknown
use but similar to one from a nuraghe in the Nurra; various
pieces of twisted bronze wire of hexagonal section; 1 wedge or
small anvil; 2 big-bladed hunting knives or daggers, very
wide and flat (one with slight medial ridge on one face), from
17–33 cm. long.
Forraxi Nioi (*Nuragus*) (Founder's hoard, seventh–sixth
centuries?)

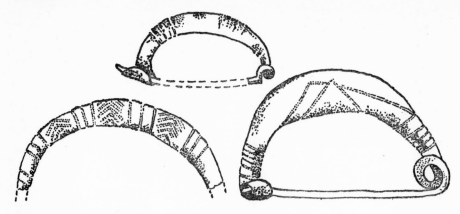

Fig. 50. Sketch of brooches from Forraxi Nioi. (After Fiorelli). 1 : 1

Contained in a huge situliform jar 70 cm. high, within a round Nuragic structure, resembling buildings at S. Vittoria and Serrucci. The large number of objects recovered included: spearheads; ferrules; 1 dagger handle; 1 votive quiver (showing a dagger on one side and 3 bolts on the other); 1 dagger casing; flanged axes; 1 socketed double-axe; 1 looped axe with stop-ridge and fragments of others; sword fragments; saw blades and files; 1 socketed sickle; big pins or bolts with decorated heads; vessels in bronze sheeting, one with spirals in relief and another with incised herring-bone design; loops and rings perhaps belonging to these vessels; a votive ship-lamp with detached bull-head prow; buttons; amber beads; lumps of bronze, iron, lead, copper and cassiterite; a small flake of gold; 2 brooches with swollen hollow bow; 2 serpentine brooches with knobbed bow; and a small hammer perhaps used for refinishing bronzes after casting.

This important hoard was thought by Taramelli to have represented a founder's collection of bronzes taken from a sacred site, perhaps the well at Santu Millanu not far away. But the character of the bronzes does not support this opinion.

Fig. 50

The brooches were almost certainly imported from Italy where the swollen bow type belongs to the eighth–seventh centuries, and the knobbed serpentine one to about 700 B C. (Some were found in Greek tombs at Syracuse dating from the early seventh century, but elsewhere they may be rather earlier. Hencken has suggested that these brooch types were spread by the Greeks.)

Monte Sa Idda (*Decimoputzu*) (Founder's hoard, seventh–sixth centuries).

This site is in the hills bordering the Campidano. The hoard was found placed in a large pot inside an even larger one, within a circular enclosure, almost surely a nuragic foundry. Cinders and ashes near by support this theory. The hoard consisted of the following: 41 axes, some still un/sharpened, including big flat axes with semicircular blades, trunnion and double/looped axes, and a socketed axe with rectangular section; 20 fragments of sword hilts and blades, some of carp's/tongue variety with hilts rather more evolved than those from Huelva, but almost surely imported from Spain; 8 daggers and sheaths; 5 spearheads with angular section; 5 sickles of simple rivetted type and ribbed blade; 7 chisels, drills and saw fragments; 11 heads of big pins or bolts; 3 rings and clamps; 3 fragments thought to be horse/bits and rein/rings; 4 bow/draws(?) or handles, ornamented with herring/bone decoration; 5 pieces of bronze vases and handles decorated with relief ornament; 1 bronze figurine; 9 copper bun/ingots, including one weighing about 12 lb., the others lenticular and of various weights.

Fig. 51 (see also *Figs. 45, 46*)

Fig. 52

This hoard is of particular importance owing to the number of Iberian objects found. These include not only the carp's/tongue swords which are a specifically western type (of 'Atlantic' origin), but also the axes of trunnion and double/looped type, and possibly some of the other objects as well. We may assume therefore that it was a founder's hoard com/

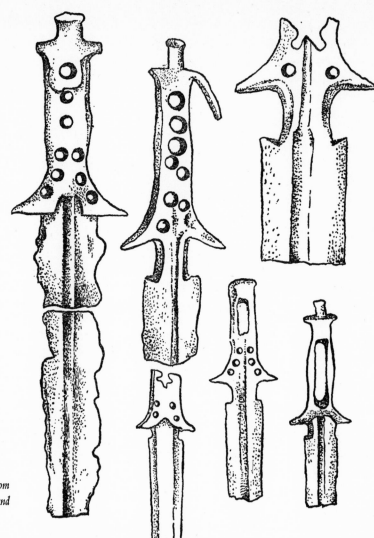

Fig. 51. Swords from Monte Sa Idda, and (top right) from Populonia

posed both of local and imported pieces. The latter evidently sometimes served as models for the local craftsmen to copy, and this may well have been the reason why they were imported in the first place.

The date of the hoard must rest on the carp's-tongue swords; these, as we have mentioned above, have a more evolved form of *ricasso* and shoulder than the Huelva examples from Spain, which have been dated by recent authorities within the period seventh–sixth centuries. Our examples may be even a century later, though. Some of the other objects may, of course, be slightly earlier or later in date than the swords.

Abini (*Teti*) (Votive hoard, seventh–sixth centuries, perhaps subsequently collected by a founder)

This hoard which certainly belonged to a sanctuary de/scribed above (page 146) may have been collected and hidden by a founder after the sanctuary had been sacked. Many of the bronzes were votive offerings and some of the stone bases in which they were fixed have been discovered. Over 250 lb. of

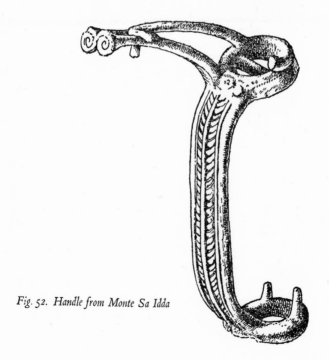

Fig. 52. Handle from Monte Sa Idda

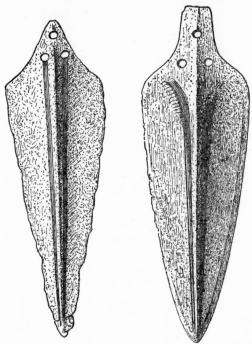

Fig. 53. Decorated dagger from Abini (Teti)

Fig. 53

Plates 52, 61

bronzes and other objects were collected; they included more than 20 statuettes of men, women and animals as well as several male and female terracotta figurines; over 100 simple swords, some which had terminals decorated with men or deer; arrowheads; spearheads; dagger blades and handles; big pins or darts; a votive quiver; bronze rings; double‑axes and palstaves; a bull's head; copper and lead cakes; bits of cassiterite and waste metal; a terracotta boat(?); a cone‑shaped ornament like one from Chilivani; and some sub‑stance which the peasants thought was incense. The site also yielded a brooch of cross‑bow type as found at Carthage in the fourth century, and a silver bracelet with bronze bell and 4 other bracelets found separately; some of these were evidently

later strays. A number of small objects, including wire armlets, a sword tip, a sheet of bronze with a row of rivets and a
piece of fused tin are in the Baux collection at Marseilles
(Musée Borely). The excavations were so haphazard that it
is difficult to get a clear idea from the accounts, but some of the
bronzes were found in the well, others in a big jar as in several
other instances, and some in holes in the ground – over 750
pieces in all.

In view of the rarity of iron objects in Sardinia, we may draw
attention to three other hoards in which iron was present.
Some at least of these iron objects may have had a bronze
casing which was precious to the founder, and this suggests
that the hoards were deposited at a time when every scrap was
treasured, perhaps after many of the metal sources and foundries had been sacked by the Carthaginians.

The hoard of Lei (Sa Maddalena) included a bronze
figurine; 3 axes; 1 socketed spearhead; a pestle; various conical
tips or ferrules; sheets of copper; decorated armlets; an ornamented dagger handle; part of a large handle; a triple-cordoned
ring; a plaque with two holes and a tang (razor?); an object
hung with shaped rings in a figure-of-eight; a bronze horn
with ball end decorated with circles and parallel lines; part
of a small hammer; and other fragments. Near-by was found a
truncated pyramid of iron, as well as a big lump of pure tin
weighing 700 grammes. This is the only instance known in
which pure tin has been found in a Sardinian hoard.

At Siniscola, various objects were found in a natural limestone cave. Amongst them were a votive bronze ship-lamp; a
bronze sword and fragments of another; part of an iron
dagger; an iron horse-bit with bronze casing; a vase with three
small feet; and an iron two-edged sword with bi-convex
blade. There were also some small bronze cups and an earthenware jar containing lumps of bronze. Some of the contents of
this hoard were dispersed and others sold.

Another hoard of the Punic period was found in a Nuragic village at Perda e Floris (Lanusei). The bronzes comprised 8 armlets and other fragments; part of a bronze statuette; awls; a small dagger blade; a broken sword; some iron rivets; broken ear-rings; and glass and amber beads of types familiar in the Tharros tombs.

Finally, there is the unpublished collection of bronze objects from Santa Maria di Paulis, now in the British Museum.

Plates 72–75 These were reputedly excavated together in 1925, and sold by a Sassari dealer in the following year. The collection con-sists of more than 70 simple, round-sectioned rings; a bronze jug with herring-bone decoration on the handle; a model bronze anchor (?); a ship-lamp; a small dagger with decorated handle; the blade of a mid-rib dagger with rivet holes; a socketed spearhead with octagonal socket; and a quantity of small fittings and bosses, including some round hanging ornaments with dangles from some large object, perhaps a stand or tripod. Possibly from the same object are 4 decorative plaques, all alike, and once no doubt fitted together to form part of a square bronze stand of a kind which finds a very close parallel in an example from Enkomi. It is therefore probably a Phoenician import from Cyprus; though what, in Cyprus, should correctly be termed 'Phoenician' and what 'archaic Cypriot' is still far from clear.

BRONZE FIGURINES AND VOTIVE BRONZES

By now it will be evident to the reader how the creative originality of the nuragic peoples was stimulated by outside influences; it is apparent in the Nuraghi themselves, in the sacred wells and the Giants' Tombs, in some of the weapons, and now, as we shall see, in the representational bronze figures. These Sardinian statuettes provide us with the most instructive information about the customs and clothing of the earlier first millennium B C, from any part of Europe outside the classical world.

More than 400 of these statuettes exist, portraying men, women, animals and, extremely rarely, a child in arms. Most of them come from the Barbagia, and many others have been lost or smelted down. The astonishing spontaneity of their expression presents us with a vivid picture of the life of the nuragic people of the eighth–sixth centuries B C both in its more barbarous aspects and in the small recurrent events of everyday life, and from the way they are portrayed we can glimpse a little of the gaiety, sorrow and dignity with which they accepted their lot.

The figurines, which range in size from 2 to 40 cm. in height, were cast in the *cire-perdue* method, or possibly from wooden models, and consequently no two are identical. Many of them still retain the lead used for fixing them to offering stands near the sacred sites, and others come from hoards, foundries, houses and tombs. Only one example has come from a stratified excavation.

They represent a wide variety of human types: musicians with triple-reeded pipes (*launeddas*) or horns, shepherds bearing animals on their shoulders, people with fruit or loaves, or with jars of water sometimes carried on the head. Leather-workers are shown carrying skins, and there are wrestlers, cripples with crutches, etc. Most of the humbler people simply wear a loin-cloth but the clothing of the warriors and the 'shepherd kings' or 'tribal chieftains', who comprise the majority of the figures, is shown in far greater detail.

Fig. 54

The 'tribal chieftains' are normally depicted in rather large bronzes. They frequently wear a rough cloth cloak and small round cap, and many carry a long knobbed stick in the left hand while the right hand is raised in prayer. The imperious severity of their expression admirably reflects the dignity of their social position.

Plate 46

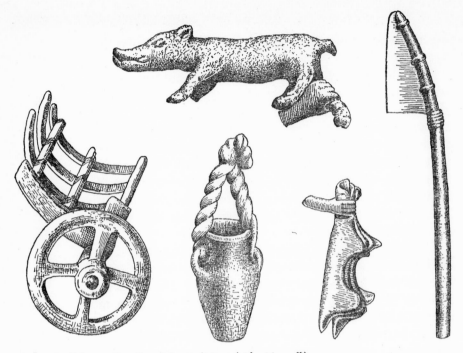

Fig. 54. Small bronzes from Santa Vittoria di Serri. (After Taramelli)

The warriors include archers, spearmen and slingers. They are often shown wearing a short tunic and vest, perhaps made of fur (this may be the *mastruca* recorded by Cicero). Occasionally these tunics are striped, suggesting that they were made with alternating strips of cloth and leather. Some wear oval leather greaves tied above and below the calf, sometimes flapping forward below the knee. A few wear apron-like skirts perhaps made of leather studded with bronze, recalling their possible prototypes in Syria and Cyprus, and by Strabo's time at least, cuirasses were made of mouflon hide. Various kinds of head-gear are shown, including helmets (made of leather?) with horns or crests, cylindrical or pointed caps and hats, often with a flap like the modern black Sardinian *berretto*. Occasionally a plumed head-dress like that worn by the dwarf-god

Plates 47–53, and 61

Bes reveals a Punic ancestry. The majority of the men are clean‑shaven though some have well‑trimmed pointed beards. Considerable interest is shown in the hair, which was usually worn short, though some warriors have long plaits hanging to the chest, or, very rarely, worn on one shoulder only.

The normal attitude is a standing one, the legs close together unlike in the archaic Greek figures, and with the right hand lifted in prayer. But there are also the water‑carriers, people bringing offerings and occasionally wrestlers and groups of standing figures.

Plates 60, 62

Their equipment is varied. Many wear gamma‑hilted daggers or hunting‑knives on the chest, and they may be armed with spears, swords, round shields and longbows. Their arrows were contained in quivers which, like the shields, were slung across the back when not in use.

Fewer women are portrayed than men. They wear dresses down to the feet and long cloaks. Their skirts may be full, and the upper part of the body uncovered. Possibly some of these figures were priestesses; at one of the sacred wells, Santu Millanu (Nuragus), a female statuette was found to have been placed under the lowest step of the stair leading to the well‑head, though originally it must have come from elsewhere as it had a protruberance at the base for fixing it in a stand. The hair was sometimes long and plaited, and covered with a hood. A few rare examples, more technically advanced, show a seated woman with, on her knee, a child or warrior son, perhaps wounded or dead.

Plate 59

Most of the clothes were presumably tied with thongs or strings, though a few stud‑like bosses may represent buttons. No brooches are shown, and this is not surprising, as the few examples known from this period (at Barumini, Forraxi Nioi, etc.) were imported types.

The stern and impassive expression of these men and women might lead us to envisage a sad and harsh life unen‑

Plates 54, 55
and 56

hanced by any lighter or gayer elements. Such an impression is, however, corrected by a glance at the animals. Yoked or single oxen, deer, sheep, goats, wild boar, dogs, pregnant sows, wolves, mouflon and a macaque monkey are all portrayed; some look stiff, flat-footed or sagging, and were cast perhaps by an unskilled founder: others are lively and naturalistic in their poses if not in their treatment, observantly and affectionately immortalised by their owners. Horses are very unusual, but there is one bronze with an archer standing on horse-back, recalling some of the gods in human form on the north Syrian bas-reliefs. (Today still at some of the village *festas* some races take place with the riders standing on horse-back, perhaps perpetuating a tradition beginning in the first millennium B C.)

Plate 61

Supernatural powers are suggested by a few figures of warriors with four eyes or four arms and several daggers or shields; most of these come from the great sanctuary at Abini. Whether these figures represent the donor's appeal to the gods for redoubled strength, or his gratitude for renewed prowess acquired perhaps after certain rites at sacred places, we may never know. It is even possible that they represent heroes like Iolaus, Sardus or Norax who we know from the classical writers were venerated as gods. The concept of doubling features is widespread in the Nuragic culture, ranging from the

Fig. 55

two faces on the candelabrum from S. Maria di Tergu to the decorative sword-terminals with two deer-heads and the pairs of animals or birds on the model ships. Such a pairing of features is known both in the bronze work of Asia Minor and the Balkans and, later, in the Celtic world. Other unusual figures include an ithyphallic flute-player and a curious man-

Plate 63

headed bull or sphinx from Nule, more fully discussed below.

Many other bronzes come from the same cultural horizon as the statuettes. There are the model ships, many of which were probably used as lamps. These have an animal-head prow,

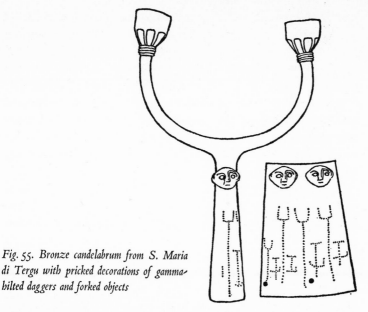

Fig. 55. Bronze candelabrum from S. Maria di Tergu with pricked decorations of gamma-hilted daggers and forked objects

generally a ram, sometimes a mouflon, or deer; and often other small decorative animals along the gunwale. A ring for suspension is also a usual feature. A number of these have been found in north Italy, at Bizenzio on the lake of Bolsena, at Castagneto and at other sites in Tuscany including Corneto and Vetulonia. One fine example, resembling a veritable Noah's ark for the quantity of animals displayed, came from the *Tomba del Duce* in Vetulonia and resembles one in the Sassari museum. This tomb is dated, on the basis of the Greek analogies of some of its contents, to well after the beginning of the seventh century. It also contained a square-mouthed socketed axe like others from the *Tomba delle tre Navicelle,* which also produced ship-lamps, this time associated with a high *aryballos* of late proto-Corinthian form, dated by Payne to 650–640 B C though this evidence only provides a *terminus post quem* as the *aryballos* could have been a local imitation.

Plate 57

177

In a hoard from Populonia a model ship was found associated with a carp's-tongue sword similar to some from Monte Sa Idda, and dated by Hencken to the seventh–sixth centuries. How much earlier these ships first made their appearance we cannot say. They may even have originated in Sardinia and then been copied in a mixed Sardinian–Etruscan setting; perhaps in Vetulonia, which was an important bronze-working centre. Deer-heads of geometric rigidity similar to those on the ships were found in a hoard at Trestina, near Città di Castello.

The proposed date for the statuettes in the eighth–sixth centuries has been confirmed by the stratigraphy of the excavations at Barumini. Here a statuette stylistically comparable with both the Abini examples and others from an orientalising culture in Etruria was recovered from behind and under the wall of a hut in Lilliu's Nuragic II, and it should belong to the third phase of the nuraghe's development (Nuragic I Upper, second-half of the eighth century until the destruction of the nuraghe by the Carthaginians). This date of Lilliu's also took into consideration a brooch of *a navicella* type (widespread in Etruria during the first half of the seventh century) from another hut of the same chronological horizon.

Plate 58

Another most interesting import from north Italy is the recently discovered and hitherto unpublished hammered bronze cauldron found on a ledge in a small cave at Gonone, on the east coast, and now in Milan. It is here mentioned and illustrated with the kind consent of the finder. This large bronze bowl has spiral-decorated handles very closely paralleled from the great hoard of San Francesco, Bologna, which included fibulae of Benacci II type (*a gomito* and *serpeggiante*). We must also remember the few brooches of north Italian type in Sardinian hoards as well as at Barumini, and the razors; all these objects together imply a commercial or piratical activity along the Tuscan coast in the eighth–sixth centuries.

Strabo referred to Sardinian piracy along this coast, and also attributed a Tyrrhenian origin to the Sardinians. As more discoveries are made on the east side of the island (the area least known from excavation) it is probable that more Etruscan and Villanovan trade objects will come to light. We already have evidence of exchanges from the brooches, ship-lamps, votive quivers and razors; there are too the oblique-mouthed jugs which are common to both regions, and the presence of *bucchero* ware of Etruscan origin in Sardinia. Pallottino has hinted that the name *Aesaronenses* for one of the tribes living on the east coast of Sardinia may share a common element with the Etruscan word *aisar,* meaning 'gods'. He also suggests that certain architectural features in rock-cut tombs at S. Andrea Priu may have imitated tombs at Cerveteri; but the Sardinian tombs are, in the light of more recent evidence, likely to be much earlier in date. On the other hand the incised drawings on the Giants' Tomb at Sulcis recalls the art of the Picene stelae.

Fig. 27

Other bronzes from Sardinia include some whose magico-religious significance cannot unfortunately be understood. There are the curious forked objects shown on some sherds from Sant'Anastasia (Sardara) and in the two bronzes from S. Maria di Tergu, near Castelsardo. One of these was evidently a candelabrum with a socket, once presumably fitted with a wooden shaft or stand. Lilliu has proposed a date for this in the seventh–sixth centuries. The socket is decorated with a pricked design of long fork-like objects and gamma-hilted daggers. Above these pricked drawings are two faces in relief, one on each side, above which the two arms of the candelabrum divide. Stylistically this object is hard to place. Such candelabra are not common in the Western Mediterranean world outside Etruria. The pricked design is hardly likely to have been conceived outside Sardinia as the dagger type is a local one. The paired faces could have been inspired

Fig. 55

Fig. 56

from various sources, but the rendering of the features is curiously similar to the imp-like face on one of two Celtic gold rings now in the Victoria and Albert Museum, London, and kindly brought to my attention by Mr J. V. S. Megaw. These were bought from an English collector in Rome in 1871 and were recorded as coming from Sardinia, and it is possible that they were found in Punic tombs looted at Tharros or elsewhere. The most likely origin for these, which were certainly made somewhere in the Celtic world, is perhaps Spain, where similar faces ornament some objects from Cadiz. Or they may have had an Italic background. That Celtic influences were occasionally felt in Sardinia need hardly sur-prise us: from the Nuraghe Losa there are inscriptions which may be attributable to Celtiberian mercenaries in the Cartha-ginian army, and it is probable that some of these men remained on in the island into the fifth century. The rings appear to belong to the fifth and late fourth centuries, the earlier being fairly close in style to the gold work from Rodenbach.

Another somewhat similar forked object, again with a small face below the arms, came from the same place, and candelabra of quite a different form, imported from Cyprus, came from S. Vittoria (Serri) and San Vero Milis. A frag-ment of another candelabrum is said to be in the unpublished hoard of Tadasune in the Cagliari museum.

Plate 63

The sphinx-like figure from Nule clearly reveals an oriental inspiration, and Pallottino regards it as further evidence of the westward spread of Asiatic motifs, emphasising that two oriental trends, Syro-Cypriot and Urartian, had met in the Greek Aegean and jointly reached Italy in the seventh century. The head-dress on the Nule sphinx or centaur seems com-parable to those of the Urartian heads on the Vetulonia caul-dron, and like other bronzes from the west Italian tombs may possibly have been made by Urartian craftsmen, or copied from their work.

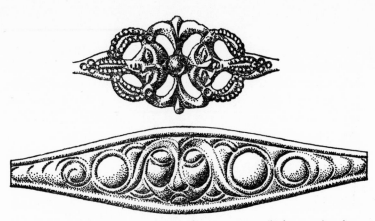

Fig. 56. Enlarged decoration on two Celtic finger-rings, reputedly from Sardinia (Victoria and Albert Museum, London)

Wheeled vehicles were evidently in use at about this period or not much later. A model chariot from near Sassari is now in the Pigorini Museum at Rome, and in a recent publication it has been compared with East Mediterranean types. Another, though different, was among the small bronzes at S. Vittoria (Serri), and we should not forget the bronze coffer-like object on wheels from Oschiri (Sassari), evidently a model.

Plate 64

To return to the bronze statuettes. They have been divided into two groups by Lilliu: the Uta-Abini group (geometrical) and a Mediterraneanised Barbaric group which is less sophisticated and includes many ingenuous figures portrayed with little skill or detail. The two stylistic groups seem to be contemporary, and as we have said above, mostly fall within the period eighth–sixth centuries or a little later. It is not impossible, however, that some figurines were imported earlier as somewhat comparable examples from Late Minoan III contexts (Syro-Phoenician) are known in Crete.

All these bronzes show such a coherent and local style that definite stylistic equations are impossible to find, but the period of their production coincides with the geometric and archaic phases of the Graeco-Italic cultures, and it must not be forgotten that small terracotta and bronze figures which may have served to inspire the Sardinian series were diffused from the Near East to Greece and Italy in the early part of the first millennium. Particularly interesting in this connection are the terracottas from Cyprus, from whence direct imports of other bronze objects are also attested from Sardinia at the same period. As Pallottino has written, 'The Sardinian bronzes fall within the ambit of the small pre-archaic plastic art of the Mediterranean, and have a partial generic resemblance with bronze figurines from Luristan, Armenia, Syria, Asia Minor, Greece, Italy and Iberia. It would be interesting to find out which area was stylistically closest . . .' Inspiration may, in fact, have come from a number of sources. As we have seen above, Phoenicians, Greeks, Celtiberians and Carthaginians could all have contributed, while Etruria, so short a distance away, was one of the most productive areas in the manufacture of small bronzes of pre-archaic type. It is not impossible too that some figures on gems from the Punic sites caught the imagination of the Sardinian bronze-workers.

Only a few Sardinian objects seem to have found their way abroad, and it is arguable that, like Etruria, Sardinia was producing metals which attracted foreign traders to set up small coastal markets. Through the medium of these traders were introduced not only improved mining techniques but also perhaps the *cire-perdue* method of casting, as well as small terracotta and bronze figurines, weapons and other trade objects. The Sardinians were receptive to new ideas which they translated into their own distinctive rendering. So long as the island shores were open to foreign trade the indigenous culture was continually enriched and rejuvenated: it was only suffo- cated when the external sources of inspiration were blocked by the Punic and Roman occupations. This would explain why the Nuragic culture never became an iron-using economy, but retained a Bronze Age tradition into the Roman period.

We have seen in a previous section that in the villages which were contemporary with the archaic forms of nuraghi at Enna Pruna and Su Guventu, pottery of Monte Claro, Ozieri, and Bonnanaro derivation continued to be made, and this situation held good until about the tenth-century or perhaps later. Until then the pottery included many carinated bowls, tripods with flat rather than rounded legs, ledge and hammer rims on large grooved jars, and incised or punctated patterns sometimes filled with red to enhance the design, in a lingering tradition of Ozieri origin.

At the same time the Giants' Tombs (which are again not closely datable) mostly contain pottery of simple forms strongly related to Bonnanaro wares. At Goronna, a number of shallow bowls and platters suitable for holding offerings were recovered.

From about the eighth century the coarse pottery in use for everyday purposes declined both in quality and form and was much less frequently decorated. On the other hand very finely made and ornamented wares inspired from examples in use outside Sardinia began to be produced for special offerings. The decoration on these pots, which are generally globular or pear-shaped in form, with several handles, and sometimes a strainer-like spout, is geometric in character, and consists of concentric circles, herring-bone incisions, comb decoration and occasionally cordons; or it is painted. Many of these elements reflect influences reaching Sardinia through trade with the outside world, especially with Etruria, which began on a larger scale with the establishment of the first Phoenician settlements in about ninth–eighth centuries. Indeed, many of the motifs on the highly decorated wares from Sant'Anastasia, the Nuraghe Lugherras and elsewhere find their closest parallels in Etruscan and Villanovan pots. The oblique-mouthed jugs (sometimes called *Schnabelkannen*) which characterise the

Plate 65

Plate 67,
Figs. 57, 58

Fig. 57. Nuragic pottery forms. (Not to scale)

Fig. 58. Decorated ware of Nuragic period from Sant'Anastasia (Sardara)

eighth–sixth centuries may perhaps have originated in Cyprus, but were widely copied in the West Mediterranean at this time.

At Barumini, which has provided almost the only stratified pottery of the Nuragic period, but which is unfortunately not yet published in detail, Lilliu found that in *Phase b* (first half of the eighth century BC) the forms were still traditional. They included carinated bowls, with handles or small lugs, hemispherical bowls, sometimes with omphalos base, and jugs with long handles from the rim to the middle of the globular body which may be ancestral to the oblique-mouthed jugs of a few decades later. Occasionally the bowls had tongue-like projections above the rim, and some lids are also known.

Fig. 58

Most of these pots were made of reddish or brown paste, rather roughly finished and badly fired, but there were a few sherds of finer black *bucchero* ware.

This is approximately the time of the richly decorated series from Sant'Anastasia, which also included one or two pots painted with yellow lines on a dark red ground.

By *Phase c* (eighth–sixth centuries BC) decorated oblique-neck jugs are not uncommon, the earlier ones tending to be more rigid and less sinuous in shape than the later ones. There are also pear-shaped jars with false strainers and decorations like the Sant'Anastasia one. Glossy black *bucchero* ware is now common, and glossy red ware is also known. Pottery lamps were found at Sant'Anastasia, Santa Vittoria and other sites, and Barumini, Losa and Sant'Antine produced pottery *pintaderas*. Tripods with round-sectioned legs sometimes date from this period, and some bowls divided inside into four segments, found at Fanne Massa (Cuglieri), Sant'Anastasia, Serra Orrios, Peppe Gallu and Goronna, are thought to be contemporary with one of the same type from this phase at Barumini. In that case, those from Fanne Massa and Goronna must be several centuries later than the rest of the finds, indicating perhaps a re-use of the tombs.

In the village of this period at Barumini carinated bowls and pots with an elbow-handle were still in use. We must also remember the enormous storage jars in which some of the founder's hoards were discovered.

Phase d (fifth century BC) at Barumini was more decadent. The high quality and decorative finish of the finer wares is no longer found. This was the early period of Carthaginian occupation, and the native peoples seem to have had to content themselves with simpler, rougher wares.

In the post-Nuragic *Phase e* of the Punico-Roman period a number of imported wares appeared. These will be described in the last chapter.

Chapter VI

The Shardana

THE PROBLEM which we must now discuss is one which has fascinated but baffled scholars for a great many years, and it would be out of place here to attempt to do more than outline its main points and difficulties.

It is well known that among the Sea Peoples who made raids on the coasts of the Mediterranean and against Egypt, and who were also employed as mercenaries in the Egyptian army, soon after the mid second millennium, were a people known as the Shardana. The fact that these people, according to Egyptian sources, came from the islands in the Mediterranean, together with the fact that their name resembles that of Sardinia, has led to the hypothesis that the connection was a real one: that many centuries before the period of the Full Nuragic culture – at its very inception in fact – either Sardinian adventurers left the island to try their luck as mercenaries; or that rather later after the final defeat of the Sea Peoples in the twelfth century, warriors displaced from another part of the Mediterranean fled to Sardinia. The first alternative would assume that the island had already become known by some such name as Sardinia: the second that the name was given to it after the domination of warrior-overlords arrived in or after the twelfth century from a land of higher civilisation in the East Mediterranean. Of these two possibilities the second seems more feasible.

If these warriors left the island with their normal equipment of weapons and armour in the fourteenth century BC, it seems strange that in no single instance has a comparable weapon been recorded from their homeland. If, on the other hand, a few dominating leaders arrived as heroes only a few centuries before the Phoenician trading-posts were established, several features of Sardinian prehistory might be explained as innovations introduced by them: oriental types of armour, and fighting equipment perpetuated in the bronze representations of warriors several centuries later; the arrival of the Cypriot copper ingots of Serra Ilixi type; the sudden advance in, and inventiveness of design of the nuraghi themselves at about the turn of the first millennium; the introduction of certain religious practices such as the worship of water at sacred wells, if this was not in fact introduced by the Phoenician settlers.

We know from classical sources that ancestor worship played an important part in the religion of the Nuragic peoples, and this practice may well have been inspired by a memory of the heroic character of their forefathers, whom they also perpetuated in the bronze figurines which, owing to increased knowledge of metallurgy, were made in large numbers by the Full Nuragic period. So far the lack of comparable weapons from the late second millennium in Sardinia need not bother us unduly if we are concerned with only a few warrior overlords. Let us, then, look at the problem more closely.

The earliest mention of these people is in the Tell el-Amarna letters, where the so-called *Srdn-w* (more usually called Shardana or Sherden) were mentioned in several letters from Rib-Addi, governor of Byblos, to Amenhotep IV (Akhenaten). This would be in about 1370 BC. These were the first of the Sea Peoples who began their raids after the collapse of the Minoan sea-supremacy.

In the time of Rameses II (1312 to 1246 BC), the Luki (Lycians perhaps of Illyrian origin) and the Shardana are again mentioned, together with various other groups including the *Šqrššw* (Sikels?). Some were used as mercenaries in the Egyptian army. Again in the reign of Rameses III, probably about the year 1191 BC, we hear of a great invasion of the Western Delta, led by Philistines, after the fall of the Hittite empire under pressure from the Indo-Europeans. In the famous inscriptions and reliefs from the temple at Medinet Habu, the Sea Peoples are referred to as coming from 'the country which came from their islands in the midst of their ocean,' (the Great Green), and from 'northern countries and their islands', etc.

The place of origin of the Shardana is therefore open to speculation. On the whole it seems most likely that these people originated in the region of Hermos (on the mainland of Asia Minor), east of the island of Chios, which may also have been included in their territory). Here Sardis and the Sardinian plain near by may preserve evidence of their name. Until recently it had been thought that Sardis was not founded until later than this date, but earlier levels are now being uncovered in American excavations. As A. R. Burn has stressed, it is strange that no traces of the Shardana occur in Greek or Hittite legends or documents, suggesting that they hardly can have come from the sphere of influence of either. They may have been pushed to the coast and islands where famine or lack of space drove them in search of adventure and expansion. An alternative theory that many of the Sea Peoples came from Italy, Sicily and Sardinia, is less easy to support. It seems more probable that some such name as Sardinia was given to the island by disbanded Sea Peoples after the great defeat under Rameses III. In view, however, of the specific mention of Shardana in the company of peoples possibly from, or giving their name to, Sicily as early as the thirteenth century B C, the alternative cannot be lightly dismissed, that adventurers from the islands and coasts of the western Mediterranean were employed either as raiders or mercenaries. The *Trs-w* (Tursci) were also mentioned as allies of the Philistines against Rameses III, but attempts to equate these people with the Etruscans (known as Tyrrhenians by the Greeks) are still not wholly satisfactory. The evidence therefore for Sikels, Sardinians and Tyrrhenians coming from the West Mediterranean, from lands already bearing their names, is to say the least, very flimsy.

In favour of the first hypothesis is the strong East Mediterranean character of the armour and weapons carried by the
Shardana. On the reliefs they are shown carrying a round
shield and a long thrusting sword. They are wearing a complicated corselet made of overlapping bands of metal or leather,
and a horned or crested helmet.

The corselet is particularly interesting. It is very similar to
that worn by the Philistines, depicted on the temple of Medinet
Habu. A corselet of plated strips, though not closely similar,
has also recently been found in the excavations at Dendra
(tomb 12) where pottery of Mycenaean II B–III A 1 dates it to
the second part of the fifteenth century BC. Two hundred
pieces of corselet armour were captured by Thothmes III of
Egypt after a battle at Megiddo against the Assyrian kings.
Its origin seems definitely Near-Eastern if not actually oriental.

The Shardana sword was an exceptionally long two-edged
bronze weapon which Breasted suggests developed from the
dagger type after the discovery of tin in Bohemia. The Philistines and their allies seem to have been among the first users
of this improved weapon, and it may have been this factor
that caused the Shardana to be so valuable as mercenaries.
The types of sword found in Sardinia have only an exceptional
length in common with the Shardana swords.

Round shields are also shown being used both by theNorth-
ern Peoples and in the bronze statuettes of Sardinian warriors.
The horned or crested helmet is sometimes depicted with a ball
decoration, but the Philistines also wore a feathered head-dress
– perhaps perpetuated in the head-dress of Sardus Pater at a
much later date. Horned helmets are worn on many of the
bronzes statuettes, and the same characteristic is found in the
West only in south Italy and Etruria.

Neither this armour nor these weapons occur in Sardinia as
early as the second millennium BC. Where we are able to date
the bronze weapons or the armour shown on the bronze

statuettes, they are several hundred years later. If, therefore, we accept the possible hypothesis that some adventurous Sar‑ dinians joined the ranks of the mercenaries in Egypt's army in the mid second millennium, or more plausibly that the Shardana left their native shores on the coast of Asia Minor to fight sometimes with and sometimes against the Egyptians, and then, disbanded, settled and gave their name to Sardinia, we must, as far as our knowledge goes at present, regard the bronze weapons known from dated archaeological contexts in Sar‑ dinia as archaic types which lingered on in the native tradition several hundreds of years after they had been in use. Moreover, all the bronze armour and arms shown on the statuettes which are of eastern Mediterranean inspiration, could equally well have come in with the Phoenicians in the course of their settlement and trade. The whole question must therefore be left an open one for the time being.

CHAPTER VII

Phoenicians and Carthaginians

THE PHOENICIAN TRADING SETTLEMENTS

AFTER NEARLY a thousand years of slow development and consolidation following her early settlement by East Mediterranean peoples, Sardinia suddenly found herself on the newly opened-up sea-routes pioneered by the Phoenicians. The Mycenaean trade in the West Mediterranean, while affecting Sicily and the Lipari islands so short a distance away, seems to have followed sea-routes which left out Sardinia, away to the north. It was only after the eighth, or at earliest ninth century that she once again came fully into the orbit of the Eastern world; then her economy, based on splendid natural resources and developed by a vigorous people stimulated by foreign technicians, responded to the full, and it is reflected in the flourishing renaissance of the Full Nuragic period.

We shall mainly here concern ourselves with the Phoenician settlements, using that term for the period before the Carthaginian military occupation after the late sixth century. (The use of the name Phoenician should, correctly, cease once the African element from Carthage was dominant and for which the term Punic is more commonly used.)

So long as the Aegean was under Minoan or Mycenaean domination, no widespread movements by the Phoenicians disturbed the more backward West; but after about 1200 BC their prospecting expeditions reached farther and farther west. The most explicit mention of their activity in the West Mediterranean comes from Diodorus Siculus who says that the Phoenicians were seeking silver, and having found it accidentally melted by forest fires in the Pyrenees, carried it to Greece and Asia. So eager were they to take all that they could load on to their ships, that when they were fully laden they even replaced the lead of the anchors with silver. 'And they prospered greatly, thanks to commerce of this kind, and sent forth many colonies, some to Sicily and its neighbouring islands, and others to Libya, Sardinia and Iberia.' Exactly when this refers to is not certain, but it is improbable that it was much, if at all, before the ninth–eighth centuries. The Serra Ilixi and other ingots of several centuries earlier, are more likely to have been shipped by Mycenaean than by Phoenician traders, unless they were brought to Sardinia by some of the Shardana; a possibility not to be discounted.

Unlike those of the Carthaginians who held Sardinia by force, the Phoenician settlements appear to have been peaceful and to have been limited to a few trading stations around the coast, usually promontories or off-shore islands which offered good beaching facilities for their boats. Other factors influenc-ing their choice were the presence of a rich hinterland (par-ticularly for metals) and of lagoons and salt marshes for netting and preserving fish by methods which are described by Pliny. The four most important of these settlements were at *Sulcis* (Sant'Antioco), *Caralis* (Cagliari), *Nora* and *Tharros*, but the dates of their foundation are still disputed, though so far no West Mediterranean colony can be proved earlier than the eighth century, and even the important site of Motya in Sicily was probably founded after the Greeks had already started colonising the east of that island, and Carthage itself (traditionally founded in 814 BC) has produced very little, if any, material as early as that date.

It is sometimes thought that two inscriptions in Phoenician characters from Nora belong to the ninth century, as their lettering is archaic. One is hardly legible and the other, which has been claimed to be a dedicatory inscription of a temple built by Phoenicians coming from Cyprus, has been compared by Rhys Carpenter to a seventh-century medallion from

Plate 69

Carthage which bears similar lettering. The earliest tombs so far discovered from Nora do not ante-date the sixth century, but the site is still under exploration, and some of it is now under the sea. Pausanias wrote of Nora as being traditionally the first of the Phoenician foundations in Sardinia, and Solinus refers to the Iberians (probably Phoenicians) coming from Tartessos under Norax. There is therefore at least a hint that Nora was founded as an intermediary port of call for ships trading with Tartessos (probably the Tarshish of Ezekiel, who refers to silver, iron, tin and lead coming to Tyre from that port, now almost certainly identified with the mouth of the Guadalquivir in Andalusia). The earliest mention of Tartessos comes from Isaiah in passages of eighth-century date. For the moment the most likely date for the foundation of Nora is in that century, but it may have been earlier. It seems to have received contingents from both the East and West Mediterranean.

Nora, on the coast some 32 km. south-west of Cagliari, was first excavated in 1889 when the chance discovery of a *topheth* led to further research in the Punic and Roman cemeteries. In 1952 work was resumed, and the inhabited area on the little peninsula was uncovered. Many Roman buildings came to light, including temples, but the early settlement seems to have been on the rocky promontory where until fifty years ago remains of Punic and Roman fortifications could still be seen. A temple of Tanit probably dates from the early fifth century and may have been built of stones taken from a dismantled nuraghe, and some houses may be as early as the seventh century. The only evidence of earlier settlement is provided by the inscription.

Caralis, or *Karales*, was probably on the headland of Sant' Elia, but no early tombs have been found there; they belong to the fifth century or later. The exact site is therefore uncertain, particularly as Cagliari has lagoons and shores which may present a rather different coast-line from that of Phoenician times, and the original settlement may have been covered by the present town. A temple of Astarte is known to have stood on Capo Sant'Elia and another on the little island of San Simone. Two cemeteries belong to the full Punic period: one in the locality known as Tuvixeddu, and the other at Predio Ibba.

Sulcis was probably founded almost, if not quite, as early as Nora, and the site must have been chosen for the rich lead deposits on the island. Random excavations have taken place here, but very little systematic work. Large cemeteries have produced a quantity of material, including eighth-century red-burnished pottery like the earliest pottery from Carthage, as well as stelae which, according to Harden, are wholly comparable in style and date to those from the Tanit precinct at Carthage. Some single-spouted lamps found in the most recent excavations at the *topheth* (further to the north) are thought to be of ninth-century date. Two vases with geometric designs (eighth–seventh centuries) were among the great quantity of material recovered: stelae, lamps and figurines, amulets and more than 300 whole urns, many of which contained burnt bones and children's teeth. These were sacrifices made to the god Mol'k, a rite which continued to be practised until stamped out by the Romans.

Tharros (Capo San Marco). Here the Phoenicians seem to have established themselves where there was already a Nuragic settlement, on an isthmus which allowed them two alternative ports. This trading post was considerably extended in the Carthaginian period. Unfortunately, in 1851 Lord Vernon, an English dilettante, made some excavations in certain tombs at Tharros which produced valuable gems and gold objects. After this a mad rush to find valuables led to the complete looting of most of the tombs, and the dispersal of the jewellery to dealers and collectors all over the Continent. Some responsible excavations have also been conducted and work is still continuing. Dr Barnett, who is studying the collection brought back to England and now in the British Museum, has informed me that at first glance none of this jewellery seems to ante-date the battle of Alalia in 535 B C after which a Punic settlement may have grown up around an earlier Phoenician nucleus. In this battle the combined Punic and Etruscan fleets defeated the Phocaean Greeks, putting an end to their dreams of territorial expansion in Sardinia, and leaving the island open to fuller Carthaginian penetration. The *raison-d'être* for the rebuilding of Tharros may have been trade with Etruria. Certainly both *bucchero-sottile* pottery and some painted Etrusco-Corinthian cups have been found at Tharros, and Punic pottery of Tharros type at Santa Cerbone in Populonia.

Of the earlier settlement, which may go back to the eighth century or so, the pottery so far recovered does not go back beyond the seventh century, and the same date is given to the scarabs. The cult of Bes, the dwarf-god, was strongly represented at Tharros, and the small figurines in his image may have been made locally or imported from Carthage. Occasionally his head-dress has been copied on native bronze statuettes.

The mutual trade and cultural exchanges between the Phoenicians and the native Sardinians provide one of the most interesting aspects of the settlement. The presence of nuraghi on some of the early sites certainly suggests that the setting-up of trading stations was effected peacefully, probably with the co-operation of the native peoples who stood to gain more from the exploitation of their island resources than from the material importations received from the more developed newcomers. It can hardly be accidental that the sudden impulse, noticeable particularly in the development of mining and metal techniques, was felt just at this period; the most convincing explanation for this would be that Phoenician miners and metalsmiths taught their own techniques to the

Plate 68

native people, and that the newly acquired knowledge lead to the tremendous material and technical enrichment reflected in the Full Nuragic period. Yet the Phoenician settlement can only have been on a small scale, as twice in the sixth century the Greeks considered colonising Sardinia.

As we have seen, there are certain architectural concepts found in some of the Nuragic buildings, particularly in some sacred wells and Giants' Tombs, which are definitely foreign to the local traditions; these, like many of the bronze figurines which show strong East Mediterranean influences, must have arrived in Sardinia at second hand, copied from Phoenician buildings in the trading posts or inspired from small objects reaching the island in the course of trade.

Among the architectural details showing Phoenician or Punic influence, we may mention the following: the carved moulding on the well at Santa Vittoria, and from some Giants' Tombs at Oragiana (Cuglieri) and Nela (Sindia); the obliquely cut stones in the façade arches of other tombs, for example Oratanda and Sas Presones (Cuglieri), recalling the similar construction of a postern gateway at Motya; a pedestal for votive offerings at Teti (Abini) which both in form and technique repeats a funerary stone from Tharros (other carved stones near the façade of the big Giant's Tomb at Biristeddu near Dorgali undoubtedly had the same inspiration). The majority of these architectural borrowings may be dated between the eighth and sixth centuries, before the Carthaginians seized the island. Some of the influences may have come directly from the East Mediterranean, and others no doubt from Carthage. They probably came in times of relatively peaceful co-existence of the Phoenicio-Punic and Sardinian peoples, though it must not be forgotten that by the ninth century some of the nuraghi were being strengthened and adapted for warfare on a serious scale, most of which, no doubt, took place between rival bands or clans who had by then begun to claim

Fig. 25e

territorial rights. But some of this rebuilding may have been in response to the threat from outside; only time and more excavation can provide the answer.

Some Nuragic bronze objects found their way into the coastal settlements before the period of Carthaginian domination. Among these should be mentioned a ship-lamp and model quivers from Tharros, a gamma-hilted dagger from the same site and some of the big pins or stiletti from both Nora and Tharros. No doubt other trade commodities included skins, hunting dogs, grain and other foodstuffs, not to mention raw metal which was probably mined by the natives under Phoenician direction.

In exchange, certain numbers of small Phoenician and Punic objects found their way into native hands. Two candle-sticks, one from San Vero Milis and the other from Santa Vittoria (Serri), may have been directly imported from Cyprus in the eighth–seventh centuries, as may also the bronze stand fittings from Santa Maria di Paulis. Bronze bells, common in tombs at Nora, Caralis and Tharros, have turned up at various native sites, including Abini, Perfugas and the Nuraghe Orolio at Silanus. Some amber, glass and iron objects similar to those from Sardinian sites have also been found in the Punic coastal regions of Etruria, and bronze razors, pendants with figure-of-eight chains, bronze vessels and other north Italian imports reached Sardinia as a result, perhaps, of the trade in Tuscan tin. A recently found antenna sword (not yet published) may have had the same origin.

Of the large quantity of gold from Tharros, very little reached the Nuragic peoples. A ring with a Phoenician design in gold came from the Nuraghe Ruinas, not far from Nuoro, and a small flake of gold came from the Forraxi Nioi hoard. Silver, too, was occasionally acquired by the natives; a bracelet with little bronze bells came from Abini, and an ear-ring was found in a re-used rock-cut tomb at Cheremule.

Scarabs have been picked up on the surface at Monte Pau (Sorso) and near the Nuraghe Luzana at Bortigali, and rockcrystal beads, like some from Nora and Carthage, from Santa Vittoria (Serri). Amber, if not local, was perhaps directly imported from Syria or Sicily, and was present in some of the hoards such as Abini and Forraxi Nioi, and an ivory pinhead from Santa Vittoria resembles some from Tharros. Bronze armlets are reported from a site near Nuragus and from the Perda e Floris hoard at Lanusei.

The PhoenicioPunic pottery presents a problem, as it is not yet possible in the majority of cases to be sure which forms came into the island in the course of early trade, and which belongs to the period of Carthaginian occupation. The dated series now being acquired from both Sardinia and Motya in west Sicily will be of the greatest value.

But it was not only in the material aspects but also in the spiritual ones that we find interaction between the two cultures. As might be expected, it is mostly the poorer culture that borrows from the richer one. The Nuragic peoples borrowed from the Phoenician amalgam of religious concepts acquired from different traditions in the lands of their origin or colonisation, translating these half understood concepts into their own idiom. So we find local versions of sacred wells and temples which had their fardistant inspiration in the Near East being built in Sardinia, and in the course of time these may gradually have rivalled the traditional places of worship before the Giants' Tombs. Ancestorworship may have given place to the worship of water – a vital necessity for the crops of a growing community. But there is nothing in the archaeological record to suggest the abandonment of a fertility cult, which began in the Copper Age and continued throughout the Nuragic, Punic and Roman periods into early Christian times. These rites may still have been practised around standing stones and stelae. Of the religious ideas which found their expression in the other temples we are ignorant, and it is doubtful if we shall ever know what they were.

At the end of the sixth century the Carthaginians occupied Sardinia by force, and the death sentence was passed on the indigenous culture.

THE CARTHAGINIAN DOMINATION

By the sixth century, not only did the Phoenician settlements need more space than was perhaps amicably granted by the Nuragic peoples, but they were also threatened with competition from the Greeks. The Phoenician colonies in the West Mediterranean were now under the leadership of the Carthaginians, following the destruction of Tyre by Nebuchadnezzar in 586 BC; the attractions of Sardinia with its great metal wealth were widely known to these peoples, as well as to the Ionian Greeks, who were advised at the pan-Ionian congress of 546 BC to unite with a fleet that would be sailing against Sardinia 'where they could be both rich and free'. But action was taken neither then nor later at the time of Darius when the possibility was again toyed with. It is possible, however, as we have mentioned before, that a Phocaean colony may have existed for a few years at Olbia, a little before the battle of Alalia in 535 BC.

At about the same time a pact of friendship was signed between the Sybarites and the Sardinians (if, as seems probable, the *Serdaioi* of the inscription recording the treaty, recently found at Olympia, can be equated with the Sardinians). The city of Posidonia was to act as guarantor. Such a pact suggests that the islanders were already well known in Tyrrhenian waters and further afield (probably as pirates as well as traders), and an alliance with them would assure safe navigation between the Sybarites and the Etruscans. Anchorage must sometimes have been sought on the east coast of the island, and the discovery of objects of mainland origin must be expected here in spite of its inhospitable character. (One such import may be the statuette of Herakles found at Posada near Olbia, and though stylistically difficult to place, perhaps of Etruscan origin.)

The Carthaginians now allied themselves with the Etrus⁄cans, with the aim of preventing any Greek colonisation. After one unsuccessful attempt when they were driven off by the local people, they succeeded after the battle of Alalia in landing in Sardinia. They then proceeded to ram all approaching ships.

At this time the Carthaginian army was reorganised by the first of the Magonids. Large numbers of mercenaries were now included in its ranks, and contingents were drawn from Numidia, Mauretania and other subject states, Celtiberians, Balearic islanders and Siciliots being among those employed. By the end of the century prolonged campaigns under Has⁄drubal and his brother led to the sacking of many of the great nuraghi such as Sant'Antine and Barumini, and from this time onwards Carthaginian control spread and strengthened. The island became increasingly important economically to the Carthaginians, and a number of new towns and sanctuaries were founded. These included *Bithia* (near Cape Spartivento), *Neapolis* (Santa Maria di Nabui), *Othoca* (in the Oristano district), *Cornus* (an agricultural centre at Santa Caterina di Pitinuri), *Bosa*, *Macopsisa* (Macomer), *Carbia* (Santa Maria di Calvia near Alghero), *Nura* (near Porto Ferro), *Herakleonis Nesos* (island of Asinara), *Olbia* (perhaps of Phocaean origin, as mentioned above, and many others, not all of which are identifiable today. The earlier Phoenician sites of Nora, Caralis, Tharros and Sulcis were enlarged and given a new importance. In time some autonomy was probably allowed, and the towns may have been ruled by *suffetes* and a senate. Some patricians farmed big estates, and indigenous land⁄

Fig. 59

owners may also have been tolerated, but all these estates had to provide a certain quota of grain annually for the army.

The Carthaginian occupation was, however, never a com‚plete one, being largely limited to the western half of the island; that is to say, to the relatively accessible terrain from a military point of view. As late as 496 B C Herodotus tells us that Ionians were recommended to emigrate to Sardinia, so the rate of Carthaginian penetration, begun in about 510 B C, must have been slow. The extent of the occupation is still not clear, for the historical sources give us too little information, and excavation has been very restricted. Certainly coastal sites were established in areas like the Gallura and in the east of the island, where no real domination may ever have been achieved, though Greek colonisation was effectively prevented. In the west, as soon as the main Nuragic fortresses had been stormed or taken by siege, the Punic occupiers brought in large numbers of Libyan slaves to repopulate some areas, and particularly to work on the farms and in the mineral and salt mines, and to help exploit such resources as grain, flax, olives, tunny‚fish, sardines, coral and wool. As early as 480 B C quantities of wheat were being supplied from Sardinia to the Punic armies.

For the next few centuries the population was ethnically mixed: indigenous Sardinians in the mountains (usually from now on referred to by their tribal names), descendants of the earlier Phoenician settlers, Carthaginians and all the mercenaries and deported peoples brought in by them.

Trading was carried on with Greeks from Massalia from the fifth century. Siciliot influences and imports are shown in the painted terracotta vases of even as early as the eighth century from the *topheth* at Sulcis, and these contacts were strengthened between 409 and 268 B C; Italiot imports, too, are not uncommon in Punic sites. It is also possible that small trading groups from Etruria established themselves in the north‚east. At the

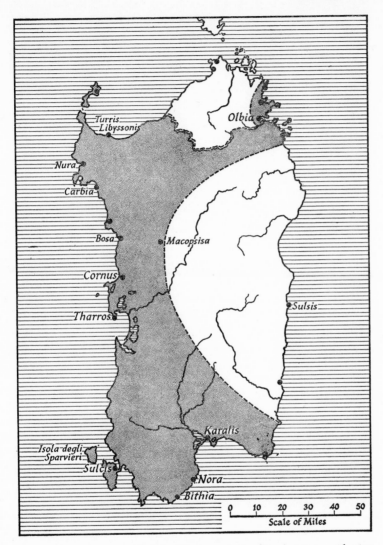

Fig. 59. Approximate area (shaded) of Punic penetration. (Based on Pesce, with minor alterations)

very start of the occupation Rome was granted trading rights, according to Polybius, provided that the business was carried out before an official. But by 348 B C when another treaty was signed between Carthage and Rome (which by now had become the strongest power in Italy), the Romans were excluded from trading with Sardinia, and had to leave within five days if accidentally driven to land there.

Houses of the Punic period are scarce in Sardinia, owing partly to the lack of excavation, and partly to their very simple construction and, often, subsequent rebuilding. Some have been identified at Nora. They were square or rectangular in plan with a beaten earth floor often provided with hollows intended for the round tips of amphorae. The walls, made of stones and pebbles bound with mud, sometimes had large pilasters set in them at irregular intervals. A few larger houses contained several rooms grouped round a central courtyard. Protocorinthian and Rhodian sherds of the seventh century were found mixed with Nuragic ware in the makeup of the floors; probably they had been found on the shore and incorporated in floors of a later date. The native huts of the Punic period around the nuraghe of Barumini date from the beginning of the fifth century. They are built with small stones bound with clay. They are round in plan, occasionally with fanshaped divisions around a circular court which may contain a well. The various rooms evidently served for different functions, such as sleeping, cooking, breadmaking (some have stone basins for the dough), extracting oil from lentiscus, and so on. The last phase of this village began in the third century, in the PunicoRoman period, when the same type of house continued to be built though trade contacts had widened. Perhaps by this time intermarriage had led to some cultural hybridism.

Punic religion is attested by a number of sacred buildings. Various high places have been found in Sardinia, of the type made with huge squared blocks forming a rectangular platform reached by a flight of steps. Here on the plastered surface the sacrifices were made and the offerings laid. Such sites are recorded from Nora (the so-called Temple of Tanit) and from Sulcis. A complex of square courtyards compose the Nora monument, which revealed several well-stratified levels. From the earliest phase came lamps and geometrically decorated pottery, which Pesce places in the eighth–seventh centuries; but the monument continued well into the Punic period. At Sulcis a *topheth* is still being excavated, while others are known from Cagliari and from Nora; in the latter place the urns contained animal bones instead of the more usual cremated human sacrifices.

Apart from the goddess Tanit (who may or may not be equated with Astarte), other gods include Bes, Eshmun, Baal, Hammon and the little-understood local god known as Sardus Pater who may perhaps be identified with Melqart, the chief god of Tyre, who was assimilated by the Greeks as Herakles; or perhaps Sardus Pater is the son of this god. According to the Greeks, he was venerated in Sardinia with the mythical name of Iolaus Pater; and Pausanias says that a statue of this god was sent by the Sardinians to Delphi. The only certain representation of Sardus Pater is on a Republican Roman coin which is iconographically of Punic type. In the course of time many small temples and sanctuaries built to various gods by groups of mercenaries and other settlers will no doubt be found.

Most of the tombs were for inhumation burials; they vary in plan from simple graves dug in the ground and lined with stone slabs, to those cut into the rock and approached either by a passage or *dromos*, or by a shaft. In the *dromos* type the rectangular burial chamber was approached from a stone-cut stairway and passage. Niches for holding lamps or incense-burners were cut in the walls of the chamber, and the body of the dead person, if rich, was laid fully clothed and bejewelled on the floor, surrounded with pottery vessels for food and drink, and weapons or toilet requisites, according to the sex. Sometimes the body was placed on a wooden bier or in a coffin made of cypress or juniper. These tombs sometimes had several chambers.

In the shaft-tombs the shaft itself is generally rectangular in section and cut with niches or steps to facilitate access. Some good examples of this type were found at Cagliari, where they belong to the fourth century or later.

The Punic necropolis at Olbia is relatively late, and the site may not have been founded (or re-founded, if a Phocaean settlement had been initiated in the sixth century) until the fourth century.

Occasionally Punic tombs of the cremation type are found, while some slab-lined tombs such as Motrox' e Bois, which are unlike the typical Punic *a cassone* tombs, were either built or re-used. At the same time the old-fashioned Giants' Tombs and even the rock-cut tombs continued to be used in many parts of the island, presumably by people of mixed Punico-Sardinian stock.

Figs. 60, 61

A quantity of Punic pottery and imported wares survive from both Punic and native sites. Beginning before the actual Carthaginian invasion, the quantity as well as the variety increased after that time. The forms have not yet been attentively studied, but some of them can be matched at Motya in Sicily where a dated series is now being obtained. The Sardinian forms include platters, whitish clay amphorae, spouted jugs, big two-handled *ollae* with concentric red stripes round the upper part on a whitish ground, handled flasks with 'mushroom' rim and the upper part painted in red glaze, various pots with painted zones or concentric rings in reddish brown, and bowls of brownish buff ware with white backing, burnished brown inside, and painted in mat red inside and

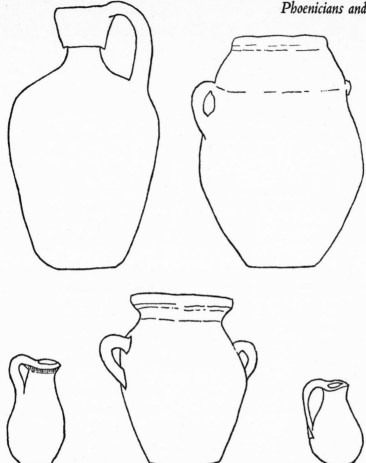

Fig. 60. Punic pottery from Predio Ibba

over the rim. Occasionally inscribed pots are also found, and some decorated moulds for making sacred bread are also Punic in origin. Few of these forms seem to be exactly similar to those from Carthage itself.

A wide variety of imported wares are found, as well as local copies of them. Of the Greek or Punico-Greek wares the

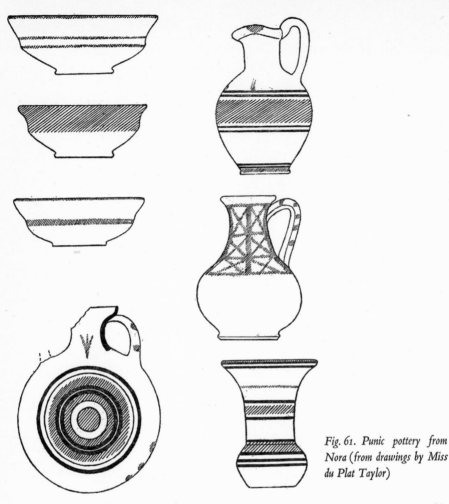

Fig. 61. Punic pottery from Nora (from drawings by Miss du Plat Taylor)

following are reported. Greek black-glaze pots of the fifth century, some black on red *lekythoi*, some very debased Corinthian ware and local imitations of Attic ware. Extensive trade with Siciliot and Italiot sites is attested by large numbers of cups, jars, platters, etc., including some south Italiot red-figure ware of the fourth–third centuries and some aryballic *lekythoi* which were earlier than the third or second century

Etrusco-Campanian pottery at Barumini. The Etruscan *bucchero* ware from Tharros, and the Etrusco-Corinthian vessels from the same site have already been mentioned, and it is interesting to note that the small terracotta figures from S. Gilla (Cagliari) also show Etruscan influence. Rhodian *amphorae* were found at the Nuraghe Palmavera.

The first Punic war ended with the Carthaginians losing Sicily and ultimately Sardinia as well. For years there was continual unrest between the ill-paid mercenaries under their Carthaginian leaders, and the national peoples of 'Nuragic' stock. Finally, in 238 BC, an appeal was made to the Romans to take over the island. This they did, in spite of its being a highly illegal action, since the Carthaginians still regarded the island as theirs. Deeply resentful of this treachery, the Carthaginians did all in their power during the next twenty years to induce the island population to rise in rebellion against the Romans. In 215 BC, under the leadership of Hamsicora, a big uprising took place, backed by a Carthaginian army which landed at Cornus under Hasdrubal. But the Romans were victorious and the island passed finally into their hands, even though there were frequent insurrections. It was not until 177 BC that the last serious stand was made by the local peoples. According to Livy, a pitched battle took place between the Romans under Gracchus and the combined Iliensi and Balari. The natives 'were repulsed and routed, and stripped of their camp: twelve thousand armed men were slain. The next day the Consul ordered the weapons to be collected, heaped up into a pile, and burnt as an offering to Vulcan.' In addition, the tribute payable by the natives was doubled.

The Punic language and culture continued to be dominant in the coastal areas of Sardinia, but the great heap of weapons symbolised the funeral pyre of the long and proud Nuragic culture.

The Romans made Sardinia a province, but no real attempt was made to colonise the island except, as Cary has emphas-ised, 'with settlements of the Botany Bay type'. Moreover, as he says, it was by-passed by the main navigation routes to the West Mediterranean, as Roman ships preferred to strike a course to the north of Corsica.

Certainly the island was not drawn into the orbit of a higher civilisation, like many barbarian lands which were conquered by the Romans, and its role was unimportant for many centuries, with its restless inhabitants subjected rather than subdued. Its post-Roman history included raids by Vandals and other barbarians, and in medieval times it was occupied by Pisans and Aragonese.

Never again did it achieve the freedom, vigour and indivi-duality of the Full Nuragic period.

Museums, Sites, and Maps

Cagliari. Museo Archeologico (Piazza dell'Indipendenza).

This is the principal collection of Sardinian prehistoric and Punic remains, and contains a huge collection, divided into three rooms dedicated respectively to prehistoric, Punic and Punico-Roman material. Most of the bronze statuettes are in this museum.

A small collection is also to be found in the Museo di Antropologia, which belongs to the Istituto di Antropologia of Cagliari University.

Sassari, Museo Nazionale G. A. Sanna. (Via Roma).

This is the second most important collection and contains some of the finds from Anghelu Ruju and S. Michele di Ozieri, and from other sites in the north of the island.

Oristano, Antiquarium Arborense (8, Via Vittorio Emanuele).

This is again, though small, an important collection, particularly for its Punic material.

An interesting private collection containing Beakers from Nuraxinieddu, etc., belongs to Prof. Giuseppe Pau, the Director, in Via Mazzini, and another collection belongs to C. Puxeddu at Mogoro.

Olbia

There is no public collection here, but the De Martis collection can sometimes be seen on arrangement with the owners.

Outside Sardinia there are also collections taking in Sardinian objects, notably at the Pigorini Museum in Rome, the British Museum (notably the finds from Santa Maria di

Paulis, and rich material from Tharros) and at the Musée
Borely, Marseilles, there are a few nuragic period pots from the
Gouin Collection.

Sites to be Visited

The best way to visit Sardinia is to hire a car and tour the
island. The main roads are excellent, and most of the smaller
roads are also good. There is, in addition, a train and bus
service.

The following list suggests a few of the sites which can be
visited from the various centres.

Alghero. Anghelu Ruju (Tenuta 'I Piani'), Nuraghe Palmavera on the road to Porto Conte.

Sassari. Rock-cut tombs at Ponte Secco, Marinaru, Su Crucifissu Mannu, and Monte d' Accoddi, are all near the road to
Porto Torres. Molafà can also be reached easily from Sassari.
The great Nuraghe of Sant'Antine (Torralba) can be reached
by rail or road from here or from Macomer. It is a few hundred
metres from the station.

Macomer. Nuraghi Losa (Abbasanta), Sant'Antine (Torralba)
and Santa Barbara (Macomer). Dolmens near Birori station.
Rock-cut tombs at S. Andrea Priu (Bonorva). Giants'
Tombs at Goronna (Paulilatino).

Nuoro. Near Dorgali various interesting sites can be seen,
including two nuragic villages (Cala Gonone and Serra
Orrios), Giants' Tombs at Biristeddu, etc., and the hidden
stronghold at Monte Tiscali (guide needed).

Olbia. Nuragic well at Golfo degli Aranci, Li Muri cist-
tombs and other sites at Arzachena, nuragic stronghold at
Cabu Abbas.

Oristano. Tharros can be visited from here, and some of the
sites between here and Macomer. The nuraghe at Barumini
can be visited either from here or from Cagliari. Not far to

the north, near S. Vero Milis, is the great nuraghe of S'Uraki, surrounded by a Punico-Roman village.

Cagliari. Caves on Capo Sant'Elia. Nuraghi of Barumini and Is Paras (Isili), the Punic site of Nora (Pula), Nuraghe Sarrok, sacred well at Sant' Anastasia (Sardara), sanctuary of S. Vittoria (Serri), and the great nuraghe of Orrubiu (Orroli).

In the Iglesiente, which can be visited from here, there is the nuragic settlement at Serrucci. The site of Sulcis is on the island of Sant'Antioco.

A Note on Maps

There are two good general maps of Sardinia which show the main physical features, towns and villages. One is Sheet 4 of the *Carta Generale d'Italia* on a scale of 1:500,000, and another (on a slightly larger scale, 1:350,000, but showing the physical features less clearly) is published by the *Automobile Clubs della Sardegna*.

Larger scale maps are the 1:250,000 sheets of the *Carta d'Italia* (sheets 32, 33, 39, 40 45 and 46), published by the *Touring Club Italiano* Milan.

The Guida d'Italia volume, *Sardegna*, published by the *Touring Club Italiano* in 1952 is invaluable for anyone wishing to do field-work.

A series of detailed archaeological maps was begun but never completed. The existing sheets are numbers 181–182, 193, 194, 195, 205, 206–208, 216 and 217 of the *Carta d'Italia* (Edizione archeologica) published by the Istituto Geografico Militare, Florence.

Selected Bibliography

Abbreviations

Arch. Classica	Archeologica Classica (Rome)
Boll. d'Arte	Bollettino d'Arte (Ministero della Pubblica Istruzione)
Bull. Pal. It.	Bullettino di paletnologia italiana (Parma and Rome)
B.S.P.F.	Bulletin de la Société Préhistorique française (Paris)
Matériaux	Matériaux pour l'histoire primitive et naturelle de l'homme (Paris)
Mon. Ant.	Monumenti Antichi (Accademia dei Lincei, Rome)
Mem. Accad. Lincei	Memorie (Accademia dei Lincei, Rome)
Not. Scav.	Notizie degli Scavi di Antichità (Accademia dei Lincei, Rome)
Proc. Prehist. Soc.	Proceedings of the Prehistoric Society (Cambridge)
Riv. Scienze Preist.	Rivista di scienze preistoriche (Florence)

General

Atti del XII Congresso Geografico Italiano (Cagliari, 1935).

Atti del Convegno archeologico in Sardegna (Reggio Emilia, 1927).

EBERT, MAX. *Reall. Vorg.* VI (1926) 94–98 and XI (1927), 208–209.

Guida d'Italia del Touring Club Italiano, Sardegna (Milan, 1952).

LA MARMORA, A. *Voyage en Sardaigne* (Paris, 1839), 2 vols. Part 3 (Turin, 1857), 2 vols. Translated into Italian and published by Il Nuraghe (Cagliari, 1928).

Le Play Society *Sardinian Studies*. Edited by G. W. Walker (1938).

LILLIU, G. 'Religione della Sardegna pre-nuragica' in *Bull. Pal. It.* N.S. XI, vol. 66 (1957), 7–96.

LILLIU, G. 'Appunti sulla cronologia nuragica' in *Bull. Pal. It.* (1941–42), 143 ff.

LILLIU, G. 'Rapporti fra la civiltà nuragica e la civiltà fenicio-punica in Sardegna' in *Studi Etruschi* XVIII (1944), 323–370.

LILLIU, G. *I Nuraghi* (Cagliari, 1962). *La Civiltà dei Sardi dal Neolitico all'Età dei Nuraghi* (RAI. Radiotelevisione Italiana, 1963).

MACKENZIE, D. 'The Tombs of the Giants and the Nuraghi of Sardinia in their West European Relations', *Memnon,* vol. II, fasc. 3. 'The Dolmens, Tombs of the Giants and Nuraghi of Sardinia' in *Papers of British School at Rome* V (1910), 89 ff. 'Dolmens and Nuraghi of Sardinia' in *ibid.* VI (1913), 127 ff.

PAIS, E. *La Sardegna prima del dominio romano* (Rome, 1881).

PALLOTTINO, M. *La Sardegna nuragica.* Il Gremio (Rome, 1950). 'El problema de las relaciones entre Cerdeña e Iberia en la antigüedad prerromana' in *Ampurias* XIV (1952).

PANNEDDA, D. 'L'Agro di Olbia nel periodo preistorico, punico e romano', *Formae Italiae,* 2 vols. (1952, 1954).

PAULY-Wissowa, *Reall. Ex. Class. Altertum,* 'Sardinia' (Philipp), cols. 2480–2495.

PERROT, G. and CHIPIEZ, Ch. *Histoire de l'Art dans l'antiquité,* vol. IV, pp. 1–118 (Paris, 1887).

PESCE, G. *Sardegna Punica* (Cagliari, 1961).

PINZA, P. 'Monumenti primitivi della Sardegna' in *Mon. Ant.* XI (1901).

ZERVOS, C. La Civilisation de la Sardaigne du Début de l'Énéolithique à la fin de la Période Nouragique. (Cahiers d'Art, Paris, 1954).

See also the museum guides to the collections at Cagliari and Sassari.

CHAPTER I THE SETTING

The Land and its Resources

CARY, M. *The Geographical Background of Greek and Roman History* (1949).

Le Play Society. *Sardinian Studies,* Edited W. G. Walker (1938).

Sardegna. Touring Club Italiano (1952).

Literary and Linguistic Evidence

PALLOTTINO, M. *La Sardegna Nuragica* (Rome, 1950) summarises what is known from ancient writers, and gives an extensive bibliography.

See also *Pausanias* X, 17, and the other sources quoted.

For Nora inscription, see PESCE, G. *Sardegna Punica.*

CHAPTER II EARLIEST SETTLERS

Some Early Sites

Li Muri, Arzachena. *Bull. Pal. It.* (1941–42), 123 ff. *Studi Sardi* VIII (1948), 35 ff.

Bressol (Catalonia). See *Los Sepulcros Megalíticos Catalanes y la Cultura Pirenaica*, by Pericot Garcia (Barcelona, 1950).

For Levkas, see Dörpfeld *Alt Ithaka*, 229 (R. 7), 237 (R. 17) and 241 (R. 24).
For platform cists in the Bari district, see *Bull. Pal. It.* XXX (1904).
For La Boussière (Var), see *B.S.P.F.* LI (1954), 281–288 and LII (1955), 666–667.

The Ozieri Culture and the Rock-cut Tombs

General. Warwick Bray. Thesis on the Rock-cut Tombs of Sardinia (Cambridge, 1962, unpublished). Audibert in *Bull. Mus. d'Anth. Préhist. de Monaco*, V (1958). Pinza, 'Monumenti Primitivi della Sardegna' in *Mon. Ant.* XI (1901). Junghans, Sangmeister and Schröder, *Metallanalysen kupferzeitlicher und frühbronzezeitlicher Boden-funde aus Europa* (Berlin, 1960). (See especially p. 150.)

San Michele, Ozieri. Bull. Pal. It. XLI (1915) 97 ff. *Not. Scav.* (1915), 124 ff. *Studi Sardi* IX (1950), 440 ff. *Arch. Classica* X (1958), 183 ff.

Anghelu Ruju. Not. Scav. (1904), 301–351. *Mon. Ant.* XIX, 409 ff. *Studi Sardi* X–XI (1950–51), 5 ff. *Studi Sardi* XVII (1959–61), 628.

'Venus' of Macomer. Riv. Scienze Preist. IV (1949), 123–133. *Bull. Pal. It.* LXVI (1957), 35. *Studi Sardi* IX (1950), 407. For Sarignano and other figures see *Bull. Pal. It.* XLV (1925), 35–61.

Santo Stefano Villamarina. Mem. Soc. Geografica Ital. XXV (1959).

San Bartolomeo. Atzeni, in *Studi Sardi* XVII (1959–61), *passim* with references, and in *Antiquity* XXXVI (1962), 143.

Capo S. Elia caves, etc. Not. Scav. (1904), 19–37.

Monte Maiore. Bull. Pal. It. (1957), footnote 52, p. 76.

San Gemiliano. Studi Sardi XIV–XV (1955–57), 13 ff., and *ibid.* XVII (1959–61), 3 ff.

Monte Olladiri (Monastir). *Studi Sardi* XVII (1959–61), 3 ff.

Santu Pedru (Alghero). *Studi Sardi* XVI (1958–59), 5. (Preliminary notice.)

Su Crucifissu Mannu. idem.

Ponte Secco and Marinaru. Studi Sardi XII–XIII (1952–54), 21–81.

Abbiu. Riv. Scienze Preist. I (1946), 106.

Busachi. Not. Scav. (1904), 209 ff.

San Benedetto. Information kindly given by E. ATZENI.

Bonnanaro. Pinza, *cit.,* col. 84 and *Not. Scav.* (1891), 324.

Is Araus. Bull. Pal. It. N.S. XI, vol. 66 (1957), 20.

S. Andrea Priu. Mon. Ant. XXV (1919), col. 76 ff.

Noeddale. Studi Sardi XII–XIII (1952–54), 82 ff., and *Riv. Scienze Preist.* XV (1960), 239.

Mores. Studi Sardi XIV–XV (1955–57), 1 ff.

Pimentel. Studi Sardi XVII (1959–61), 189–90. See also *Iraq* XXII (1960), 105 ff., and *ibid.* XV, part I (1953).

Nuraxinieddu. Pau collection at Oristano. See *Studi Sardi* XVII (1959–61), 192.

Cuguttu. Not. Scav. (1909), 100–108.

For tortoise beads, see Arnal in *B.S.P.F.* (1954), 255 ff.

Monte d'Accoddi. Riv. Scienze Preist. VIII (1953), 199 ff. *Bull. Pal. It.* N.S. VIII, part V (1953), 174. *Studi Sardi* XIV–XV (1955–57), 196. Recent numbers of *Fasti Archeologici, Studi Sardi* for subsequent notes. For *Maltese* cultures, see Evans, *Malta* (London, 1959). For *Sicily,* see Bernabò Brea, *Sicily before the Greeks* (London, 1957) and Tinè in *Bull. Pal. It.* LXIX (1960), 8–10.

For Beakers, see M. A. Smith in *Proc. Prehist. Soc.* XIX (1953), 95 ff., and Alberto del Castillo Yurrita, *La Cultura del vaso campaniforme Su Origen y extensión en Europa* (Barcelona, 1928).

The Bonnanaro Culture

Fanne Massa (Cuglieri). *Not. Scav.* (1918), 312 ff.

S'Orreri. Bull. Pal. It. (1884), and *Matériaux,* 3rd S. vol. 1 (1884).

Serbariu. Pinza, 'Monumenti primitivi della Sardegna' in *Mon. Ant.* XI (1901).

Punta Niedda. Riv. Scienze Preist. I (1946), 105.

Genna Luas. Not. Scav. (1891), 416–418.

Su Moiu. Riv. Scienze Preist. XIII (1958), 213.

Villamassargia. Bull. Pal. It. N.S. XI, vol. 66 (1957), note 52, p. 75.

Cuccuru Nuraxi (Settimo San Pietro). *Studi Sardi* XIV–XV (1955–57), 94 ff.
Trapani (Sicily). *Annales de Géologie et de Paléontologie* by Antoine de Gregorio. 4th appendix to Sicily (Palermo, 1928).

The Monte Claro Culture

Villa Claro. Not. Scav. (1904), 209 ff.

San Gemiliano and Monte Olladiri. Studi Sardi XVII (1959–61), 3–216.

Enna Pruna and Su Guventu. Studi Sardi XVI (1958–59), 3 ff.

Is Cresieddas. Studi Sardi XVII (1959–61), 208.

Is Ruinalis de Segavenu. ibid.

Sa Corona. ibid.

Simaxis. ibid., p. 279 ff.

Sa Duchessa. Studi Sardi XVI (1958–59), 3 ff.

CHAPTER III MEGALITHIC TOMBS AND STANDING STONES

The 'Dolmens'

General. MACKENZIE, D. *Papers of the British School at Rome* V (1910), 89 ff., and VI (1913), 127 ff. *Studi Sardi* VIII (1948), 43 ff. and *ibid.,* IX (1950), 439. *Bull. Pal. It.* LXVI and LXVIII. Listed with references. *Birori. Bull. Pal. It.* XXXII (1906), 268–71. *Cannigheddu e S'Ena* (Abbasanta). *Not. Scav.* (1916), 255. *Gallura, Bull. Pal. It.* (1941–42), 123 ff.

See also for:
Corsica. Bull. Pal. It. LIII (1933), 1–28 and references.
Malta. Proc. Prehist. Soc. XXII (1956), 85 ff., and for a recent discussion of the Tarxien Cemetery culture, see *Antiquity* XXXV (Dec. 1961), 303, and *Proc. Prehist. Soc.* (1961).
Catalonia and the Pyrenees. Pericot y Garcia, *Los Sepulcros megaliticos Catalanes y la Cultura Pirenaica* (2nd edition 1950).
Otranto. Bull. Pal. It. XXXVI (1910), 26–32, 86–95.

The Giants' Tombs

MACKENZIE, D. Papers in: *Ausonia* III (1908), 18–48 and *Papers of British School of Rome* V (1910), 89 ff., and VI (1913), 127 ff.

LA MARMORA, A. *Voyage en Sardaigne,* II (1857).

See also bibliography on following tombs:
Goronna. *Studi Sardi,* VIII (1948), 43 ff.
Domu S'Orku (Siddi). *Not. Scav.* (1841), 137.
Scusorgiu (Gesturi). *Not. Scav.* (1940), 23.

Sas Presones (Cuglieri). *Studi Sardi*, XIV–XV (1960), 228.
Pedras Doladas (Scanu Montiferru). *ibid.*, 225.
Sos Ozzastros (Abbasanta). *Not. Scav.*, 1916, 258.
Rio di Palmas (Sulcis). *Bull. Pal. It.* (1906), 78 ff.
Bruncu Espis. *Not. Scav.*, (1927), 360.
Mesu Enas (Abbasanta). *Not. Scav.*, (1915), 112.
Orrida (Sennori). *Riv. Scienze Preist.*, XV (1960), 238.
S'Azzica (Abbasanta). *Not. Scav.*, (1915), 113–114.
Las Plassas. *Not. Scav.*, (1943), 170 ff., 181–2.
Preganti (Gergei). *Studi Sardi*, VII (1947), 250.
Oragiana (Cuglieri) and Nela Sindia. *Studi Sardi*, XIV–XV (1960), 264.
Pedra Lada (Ozieri). *Studi Sardi*, IX (1950), 443.
Biristeddi (Dorgali). *Not. Scav.* (1933), 357.

Miscellaneous Long Cists

Domusnovas Canales. Not. Scav. (1915), 118–119.

San Giuliano (Alghero). *Riv. Scienze Preist.* XV (1960), 237.

Nerbonis (Gesturi). *Not. Scav.* (1940), 237.

Ena' e Muros (Ossi). *Studi Sardi* XIV–XV (1955–57), 9–70.

Senorbii. Not. Scav. (1931), 77 ff.

Bopitos (Laerru). *Not. Scav.* (1915), 395.

Sardara. Bull. Pal. It. (1914), 99 ff.

Motrox'e Bois. Studi Sardi XIV–XV (1955–57), 9–70.

San Gemiliano. Studi Sardi XVII (1959–61), 3 ff.
See also Panedda, 'L'Agro di Olbia . . .' I, p. 86, and *Not. Scav.* (1931), 78.
The Beaker grave at Nuraxinieddu near Oristano has been mentioned above, p. 219.

Standing Stones and Stone Settings

Listed in *Bull. Pal. It.* 66 (1957), 92–95, footnote 242.
See also La Marmora, Voyage II, *passim, Studi Sardi* XIII, footnotes
pp. 55–56.

CHAPTER IV THE NURAGIC CULTURES:
BUILDINGS

The Nuraghi

A full bibliography of the nuraghi can be found in two works by
Lilliu: *I Nuraghi* (Cagliari, 1962), which describes many, but not all
of the principal nuraghi, and 'Il Nuraghe di Barumini e la stratigrafia
nuragica', in *Studi Sardi* XII–XIII (1952–54), 90–459. See also
Panedda, 'L'Agro di Olbia . . .', and *Studi Sardi* XIV–XV (1955–
57), 55 ff.

For the nuraghi mentioned in this chapter, see:

Sant'Antine. *Mon. Ant.* (1939) XXXVIII, col. 57. *Studi Sardi* VII
(1947), 9–25. *I Nuraghi* p. 108 ff.

Barumini. *Studi Sardi* XII–XIII (1952–54), 90 ff. For revised dating
see Radiocarbon Supplement to the *American Journal of Science* II,
1960, 10 (Report from Copenhagen).

Losa. *Not. Scav.* (1916), 235 ff. *Studi Sardi* XII–XIII (1952–54), 111.
I Nuraghi, 101–105.

Santa Barbara, Macomer. *I Nuraghi*, 113–115.

Nuraghe Lugherras. *Mon. Ant.* XX (1910), cols. 9–90, and *I Nuraghi*,
105–107.

Peppe Gallu. *Riv. Scienze Preist.* XIV (1959), 59 ff.

Palmavera. *Mon. Ant.* XIX (1909).

For Corsican 'torre', see *Gallia* (Préhistoire) I (1958), and 'Filitosa et son contexte Archéologique' in *Monuments et Mémoires* (Foundation Eugène Piot) (L'Académie des Inscriptions et Belles-Lettres) vol. 52 (1961).

For 'hideouts', see *Diodorus Siculus* Book V, 15.

For Sa Corona, Villagreca, see *Studi Sardi* XVII (1959–61), 208.

Bronze Ingots

Serra Ilixi. *Bull. Pal. It.* XXX (1904), 85 ff.

Sant'Antioco, Bisarcio. *Arch. Classica* X (1958), 192.

Assemini. Mentioned only in *Studi Sardi* XII–XIII (1955), 173.

See also C. F. A. SCHAEFFER, *Enkomi-Alasia* (Paris, 1952), 28 ff.

BASS, G. 'The Cape Gelidonya Wreck', in *American Journal of Archaeology*, vol. 65, no. 3. (July, 1961), 271 ff. (Preliminary report).

Buchholz, in *Prähistorische Zeitschrift*, XXXVII, 1–2 (1959), 1–4.

Sacred Wells and Springs

List of known sacred wells in *Studi Sardi* XIV–XV (1955–57), 283.
List of known nuragic springs in *Bull. Pal. It.* LXVI (1957), 72–73.
Su Tempiesu (Orune). *Studi Sardi* XIV–XV (1955–57), 283.
Sant'Anastasia (Sardara). *Mont. Ant.* XXV (1918), col. 36 ff.
S. Vittoria di Serri. *Mon. Ant.* XXIII (1914), col. 313 ff., and *Not. Scav.* (1922), 296.
See also Panedda, 'L'Agro di Olbia . . .', *passim,* and Zervos, *Civilization.*

Temples

Serra Orrios. Boll. d'Arte (1937), 198 ff. *Studi Sardi* VII (1947), 241–42.

Esterzili. Studi Sardi VIII (1948), 313 ff., and *ibid.* XIV–XV (1955–57), 65 ff.
See WOODHEAD, A. G. *The Greeks in the West* (London 1962) and DUNBABIN, T. J., *The Western Greeks* (Oxford, 1948).
See also Meloni in *Studi Sardi* VI, 43 ff.

Villages, Citadels and Sanctuaries

Carta Archeologica. The published sheets give details of a number of sites, but the series is incomplete and out of date.

Ausonia III (1908), 18–48.

Serrucci. Mon. Ant. XXIV (1917).

S. Vittoria di Serri. Mon. Ant. Not. Scav. (1922), 296. XXXIV (1931), col 5 ff. *Ibid.* XXIII (1914), col. 313 ff.

Monte Tiscali. Not. Scav. (1933), 353.

Cala Gonone, Dorgali. *Boll. d'Arte* (1927), 476. *Not. Scav.* (1933), 370 ff.

Cabu Abbas. Zervos, p. 89 ff., and Panedda, 'L'Agro di Olbia nel periodo preistorico, *Formae Italiae* (Rome 1954), 71–77.

Abini (Teti). *Not. Scav.* (1931), 45–77.

Serra Orrios. Boll. d'Arte. (1937), 199 ff. *Bull. Pal. It.* V–VI (1941–42), 169. *Studi Sardi* VII (1947), 241–42.
For S. Nicolò (Gerrei) votive column with trilingual inscription, see *Corpus Inscriptionum Semiticarum,* vol. I, no. 143.

CHAPTER V THE NURAGIC CULTURE:
METALWORKING AND POTTERY

Mining, Smelting and Casting

RELLINI, U. 'Miniere e fonderie d'età nuragica in Sardegna', in *Bull. Pal. It.* XLIII (1923), 58 ff.

'Giacimenti di minerali in Sardegna', in *Atti del XII Congresso Geografico Italiano* (Cagliari, 1935).

Sardegna Romana, Istituto di Studi Romani (Rome, 1939) Vol. II, 19 ff.

For moulds, see *Bull. Pal. It.* XLII (1916–17), 3 ff.

Foundry at Ortu Commidu (Sardara) *Mon. Ant.* XXV (1918), 107, and new interpretation in *Studi Sardi* XII–XIII (1952–54), 104.

Weapons, Implements and Hoards

Hoards, E. Birocchi, 'I Ripostigli nuragici e le panelle di rame grezzo', in *Studi Sardi* I (1934), 37 ff.

Nule. *Bull. Pal. It.* XLVII (1927), 159–165.

Monte Arrubbiu. *Mon. Ant.* XXXI (1926).

Chilivani. *Bull. Pal. It.* XLIII (1923), and *Annali della Facoltà di Lettere, Filosofia e Magistero dell'Università di Cagliari,* XXI (1953), 23.

Forraxi Nioi. *Mon. Ant.* (1901) and *Not. Scav.* (1882), 308.

Monte Sa Idda. *Mon. Ant.* XXVII (1921), col. 5 ff., and Hencken, 'The Carp's tongue swords in Spain, France and Italy', in *Zephyrus* VII–2 (1956).

Abini. *Not. Scav.* (1878) 244, and *Not. Scav.* (1931) 45 ff.

Lei (Sa Maddalena). *Not. Scav.* (1890) 334–336.

Siniscola. *Not. Scav.* (1892) 291–2.

Perda e Floris (Lanusei). *Not. Scav.* (1883), 357.

Uta. *Boll. Arch. Sard.* III, 186.

For Huelva, see *Ampurias* II (1940), 85–143.

(Note that a few objects from hoards of Forraxi Nioi and Teti are in the collection at the Musée Borely, Marseilles).
For dating of Cypriot objects in the west, see Mrs. J. M. Birmingham's thesis cited in the bibliography for *Figurines and votive bronzes.*

Bronze Figurines and Votive Bronzes

LILLIU, G. *Scultura della Sardegna Nuragica* (1956).

PALLOTTINO, M. *The Etruscans, passim,* and *La Sardegna Nuragica.*

PESCE, G. *Ancient Bronzes from Sardinia* (Arts Council, 1954).

Antiquity and Survival (The Hague, 1955).

For *S. Maria di Tergu* candelabrum, see *Studi Sardi* VIII (1948), 5 ff. and 19 ff.

Nule 'sphinx', see *East and West* (1958); and see also 'Urartian Bronzes in Etruscan Tombs' in *Iraq* XVIII, 2.

Bronze models of wheeled vehicles. See *Proc. Prehist. Soc.* (1960), 50 ff.

Cyprus terracotta figurines. *Swedish Cyprus Expedition* (Stockholm) vol. II, plates CLXXXIX–CCXXXVIII.

See also Mrs. J. M. Birmingham's unpublished M.A. thesis for London University 1959: 'The archaeology of Cyprus from 1200–600 BC.' (Institute of Archaeology). Here she suggests a rather different dating from Gjerstadt, and claims that Cyprus trade with the west Mediterranean probably began at the end of the ninth century BC.

Pottery

Enna Pruna and Su Guventu. *Studi Sardi* XVI (1958–59), 3 ff.

Goronna. *Studi Sardi* VIII (1948), 43 ff.

Sant' Anastasia (Sardara). *Mon. Ant.* XXV (1918), col. 33 ff.

For Barumini and the other reports on nuraghi, see the bibliography for Chapter IV.

CHAPTER VI THE SHARDANA

BONFANTE, G. 'Who were the Philistines?' in *American Journal of Archaeology*, L, April–June (1946), 251–262.

BURN, A. R. *Minoans, Philistines and Greeks* (London, 1930).

PALLOTTINO, M. *The Etruscans* (Penguin Books 1955). (First Italian edition 1948).

PORRO, G. G. 'Influssi dell'Oriente pre-ellenico sulla civiltà primitiva della Sardegna'. in *Atene e Roma*, XVIII (1915), 162 ff.

TARAMELLI, A. in *Bull. Pal. It.* XXXIX (1914), 107 ff.

WAINWRIGHT, G. A. 'The Teresh, the Etruscans and Asia Minor', in *Anatolian Studies*, IX (1959), 197 ff.

WAINWRIGHT, G. A. 'Some Sea Peoples' in *Journ. Egyptian Arch.* 47 (1961), 71 ff.

For Dendra, see *Journ. of Hellenic Studies* (Archaeological Reports 1960–61), pp. 9–10.

CHAPTER VII PHOENICIANS AND
CARTHAGINIANS

The Phoenician Trading Settlements

CARPENTER, RHYS. 'The Phoenicians in the West', in *American Journal of Archaeology*, 1957.

HARDEN, D. B. *The Phoenicians* (London, 1962).

Diodorus Siculus V, 35, 5.

LILLIU, G. 'Rapporti fra la civiltà nuragica e la civiltà fenicio-punica in Sardegna', in *Studi Etruschi* XVIII (1944), 321 ff.

PESCE, G. *Sardegna Punica* (Cagliari, 1961) with references.

See also Culican, W. 'Essay on a Phoenician Ear-ring', in *Palestine Exploration Quarterly*, July–Dec. (1958), 90 ff.

The Carthaginian Domination

ALBRIGHT, W. F. 'The Role of the Canaanites in the History of Civilization', in *Studies in the History of Culture* (1942), 11–50.

LEVI, D. 'Le necropoli puniche di Olbia', in *Studi Sardi* IX (1950), 5–120.

LILLIU, G. 'Le stele puniche di Sulcis', in *Mon. Ant.* XL (1944). 'Rapporti fra la civildtà nuragica e la civiltà fenicio-punica in Sardegna', in *Studi Etruschi* XVIII (1944), 321 ff.

PAIS, E. 'La Sardegna prima del dominio romano', in *Mem. Accad. Lincei* III (1881).

PANEDDA, D. 'Olbia nel periodo Punico e Romano', *Formae Italiae* (Rome, 1953).

PESCE, G. *Sardegna Punica* (Cagliari, 1961). *Nora. Guida degli Scavi* (Cagliari, 1957).

TARAMELLI, A. 'Ricerche ed esplorazioni nell'Antica Cornus', in *Not. Scav.* (1918), 285 ff.

WARMINGTON, B. H. *Carthage* (London, 1960), *passim*.

See also the Barumini report in *Studi Sardi* XII–XIII (1952–54), and the Predio Ibba necropolis (S. Avendrace) in *Mon. Ant.* XXI (1912), cols. 9–182.

For *Sardus Pater,* see Pausanias X. 17.1 and *Atti del Convegno arch. in Sardegna* (1926), 103.

For Roman campaign under Gracchus, see Livy, Book XLI.

For discussion of *Serdei,* see P. Zancani Montuoro 'Sibariti e Serdei', in *Rendiconti (Accad. Naz. dei Lincei)* Series VIII. vol. XVII (1962).

I wish to thank the undermentioned for placing at my disposal photographs used in the plates: Signor Enrico Atzeni, 2, 3, 10, 18, 21 and 28; Professor C. Zervos, 11, 12, 17, 23, 25, 31, 38, 40, 42, 43, 62, 63, 64, 66 and 67; Alinari, 1, 6, 32, 33, 34 and 45; the Soprintendenza alle Antichità, Cagliari, 7–9, 13, 22, 24, 50 52, 55, 69, 70 and 77; the Istituto di Antichità Sarde dell'Università di Cagliari, 39; the Ministero della Pubblica Istruzione (Direzione Generale delle Antichità e Belle Arti), 51, 57 and 61: the Soprintendenza alle Antichità, Syracuse, 58; the Soprintendenza alle Antichità d'Etruria, Florence, 47; the Museum authorities at Sassari, 4, and at Cagliari, 5; Messrs Dachena and Dott. Ercole Contu, 15 and 16; the Touring Club Italiano, 30 and 71; the Director of the Musée Borely, Marseilles, 65 and 68; Bromofoto, Milan, 35–37; the Director of the Nationalmuseet, Copenhagen, 48 and 49; the Trustees of the British Museum, 72–76; Mr Edwin Smith, 44, 46, 53, 54, 56, 59 and 60; Mr John Fletcher, 14; Mr John Guthrie, 41; Professor A. W. Lawrence, 27 and 29.

The geological map, Fig. 2, is reproduced from D. S. Walker: *The Mediterranean Lands* (Methuen) by kind permission of the author and publisher. The other maps were drawn by Mr H. A. Shelley.

1

2, 3

4

5

6

7 8 9

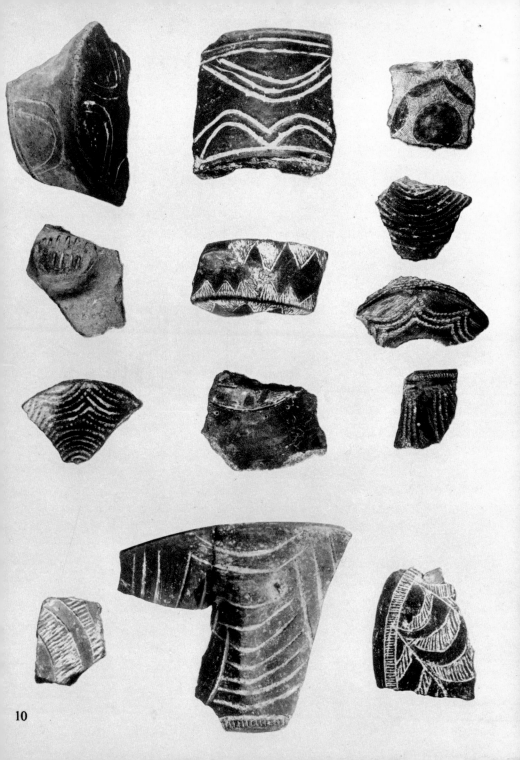

11

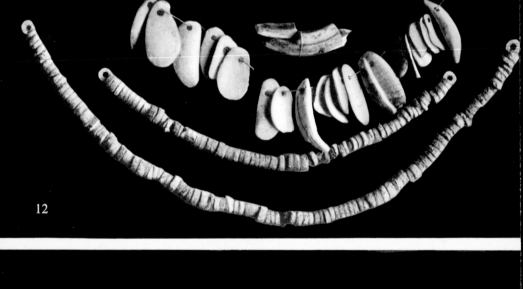

12

14

15

16

17

18

19

20

21

26

27

28

29

30

31

32

33

34

35

36

37

41

42

43

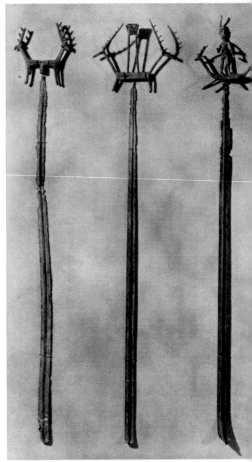

44

45

46

47

48

49

50

51

52

53

54

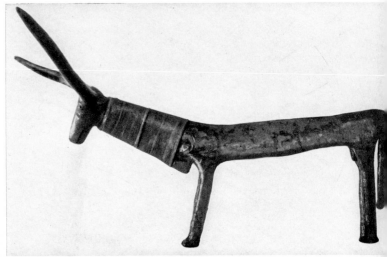

55

56

57

58

59

60

61

62

64

65

66

67

68

69

70

71

72

73

74

75

76

77

Notes on the Plates

1 Characteristic Sardinian landscape.

2, 3 Pyxis of Ozieri ware from near Oristano, showing decoration on base and sides. H. 5 cm.

4 Vase from S. Michele di Ozieri. Sassari Museum.

5 Marble statuette from Senorbì. H. 44 cm. Cagliari Museum.

6 Statuette from Porto Ferro. H. 32 cm. Sassari Museum.

7-9 Three views of the 'Venus' from the rock shelter of S'Adde, Macomer. H. 13.5 cm. Cagliari Museum.

10 Pottery of Ozieri type from San Gemiliano (Sestu). Cagliari Museum.

11 Interior of a tomb at Anghelu Ruju showing carved bull's heads.

12 Necklace of limestone and shell beads from Tomb I at Anghelu Ruju. Cagliari Museum.

13 Whetstone from Anghelu Ruju (Tomb XIII) in its case decorated with a ring pattern. The case also has two holes which correspond with those on the whetstone. Perhaps they were once fixed with rivets. L. 14 cm. over all.

14 Entrance to chambers of rock cut tombs at Su Crucifissu Mannu, near Sassari.

15 Bowl with Beaker ornament from Marinaru (Sassari). H. 7 cm.

16 Beakers from Marinaru (Sassari). H. 8 cm. and 12 cm.

17 Interior detail of the roof of a tomb at S. Andrea Priu, showing architectural details copied in stone.

18 Rock-tomb of Pimentel showing incised designs over the entrance. These designs are almost certainly of East Mediterranean origin.

19 General view of Monte d'Accoddi, near Sassari, showing ramp.

20 Monte d'Accoddi. Detail of building stones as revealed in a test excavation. The depth of soil which has accumulated against the monument is clearly visible.

21 Beaker pottery from a 'fossa' grave at Nuraxinieddu, Oristano. Above: H. 10 cm. Below: H. 11.5 cm.

22 Eneolithic pot with unusual 'pocked' design from Bagno Penale, Capo S. Elia, Cagliari.

23 Pot of Monte Claro type from tomb of Villa Claro. H. 32 cm.

24 Beaker mug from Cuguttu. The decoration is white-filled. H. 12 cm.

25 Pot of Bonnanaro type from the type site. H. 13 cm.

26 Dolmen by Birori station, near Macomer.

27 Giants' Tomb at Imbertighe. Detail of façade showing carved slab and entrance. The stone is about 3 metres tall.

28 Giants' Tomb at Is Concas, Quartucciu. This is an excellent example and shows the monumental façade and forecourt.

29 Carved stone at Biristeddu (Dorgali). This, with another similar stone, evidently formed part of the façade and almost certainly shows Punic influence.

30 Some *baetyls* which originally came from near a Giants' Tomb at Sa Perda Longa, near the Nuraghe Corbos. They are now arranged outside the church of San Lorenzo, Silanus.

31 Copper ingot from Serra Ilixi.

32 View of interior roofing showing *tholos* construction at Nuraxi de is Paras (Isili).

33 Bronze model of a nuraghe from Olmedo. H. 25.8 cm.

34 The doorway of Nuraghe Paddaggiu (Castelsardo).

35 Nuraghe Santa Barbara, Macomer.

36 Nuraghe Sant'Antine, Torralba.

37 Nuraghe Su Nuraxi, Barumini. View of the nuraghe and the village from the north-east.

38 Passage along the inside of the nuraghe at Sant'Antine, Torralba.

39 Air view of Su Nuraxi, Barumini.

40 Su Lamarzu, Rebeccu. Entrance to the well, showing paved entrance flanked by benches.

41 View of one of the temples at Serra Orrios, Dorgali. This shows the curved stone lintel over the entrance, a feature which is also found in some of the Giants' Tombs. It is also possible to see the round 'boss' thought to represent a 'breast' on the left frontal wall.

42 Huts grouped round a village street at Serra Orrios, Dorgali. A well can be seen in the left foreground.

43 Santa Vittoria di Serri. View from behind the well (once covered by a cupola), showing steps leading down from rectangular courtyard.

44 Votive swords with decorative terminals of men and deer. From Santa Vittoria di Serri. Length of swords about 1.3 metres.

45 Decorative terminal of big votive sword from Padria (Sassari).

46 Tribal chieftain wearing cloak over short tunic. He carries a wide-bladed sword in his right hand and wears a gamma-hilted dagger on his chest. From Monte Arcosu, near Uta.

47 Statuette of warrior wearing horned helmet, and carrying his shield on his back. Museo Archeologico, Florence.

48, 49 Bronze statuettes acquired from an art dealer in Paris. Now in National museet, Copenhagen. Heights 17 cm. (48) and 20.4 cm. (49).

50 Statuette of a bearded man offering his bowl. Found at Villacidro. H. 12.5 cm.

51 Small statuette of unknown provenance. H. 17.5 cm. This figure represents the less rigid of the two styles found in Sardinian plastic art.

52 Archer from Abini (Teti). H. 18 cm.

53 Archer wearing unusual type of tunic and helmet. H. 17 cm. Found at Santa Vittoria di Serri.

54 Bronze ox from S. Vittoria di Serri. L. 9 cm.

55 Standing bull from S. Vittoria di Serri. L. 14 cm. This figure and the last are in contrasting styles.

56 Bronze model boat containing a macaque monkey. Existing length 13 cm. The provenance of this is not known for certain, but it probably came from Baunei.

57 Model ship. Perhaps these were used as lamps. This example comes from Bultei.

58 Hammered bronze cauldron. Found at Cala Gonone. Diam. at rim 27.5 cm. H. 19.5 cm. It has an irregular squarish hole on the carination. Probably an import from North Italy.

59 Mother and child. From S. Vittoria di Serri. H. 11 cm. Note the mother's right hand lifted in prayer. Several other mother-and-child statuettes are known from Sardinia.

60 Wrestlers. From Monte Arcosu, Uta. H. 10 cm. L. 15.5 cm.

61 Warrior with two pairs of eyes and arms and two shields. From Abini (Teti). H. 19 cm.

62 Two warriors. We do not know what their attitudes are intended to convey. From Monte Arcosu, near Uta.

63 Sphinx-like bronze figure (? a bull) with human head, found at Santu Lesci, near Nule. L. 18.5 cm. Perhaps of Urartian workmanship.

64 Bronze model of a wheeled coffer found at Oschiri. L. 14.5 cm. Perhaps imported from Cyprus.

65 Small pots of the Nuragic period now in the Musée Borely, Marseilles.

66 Four-handled pot with unusual impressed decoration of Nuragic period. From Nuraghe Lugherras. H. 17 cm.

67 Decorated vase with double handles from S. Anastasia (Sardara). H. 18 cm.

68 Small wide-lipped jug from Tharros. Now in the Musée Borely, Marseilles.

69 A Phoenician inscription from Nora. The first five letters of the third line are thought to represent the sounds *ba Shardàn* ('in Sardinia'). The inscription is on a block of local sandstone a little more than 1 metre high.

70 Inscription to the three gods Amun-ra, Mut and Khonsu, from Tharros. Now in the Musée Borely, Marseilles. This is a Phoenician or Punic copy of an Egyptian original and belongs to about the seventh-sixth centuries B C.

71 Punic stele from Sulcis. Fifth century B C.

72 Bronze dagger from S. Maria di Paulis. Over-all length 12.2 cm. (British Museum, London).

73 Bronze dagger from S. Maria di Paulis. Over-all length 16 cm. (British Museum, London).

74 S. Maria di Paulis. Bronze jug found with the objects shown in Plates 73–75. Some at least of these objects were probably imported from Cyprus. H. 19 cm. (British Museum, London.)

75 Bronze mounts and rings from S. Maria di Paulis. (British Museum, London).

76 Trilingual inscription (in Greek, Punic and Latin) from San Nicolò at Gerrei, dedicated to Merres. Aesculapius and Esmus by one of the slaves of the salt-workers. This was found in a sanctuary associated with a therapeutic well and belongs to the early second century B C.

77 Bronze head of a bull, found at Orani in 1873 and probably of the Punic or early Roman period. This may represent the last lingering tradition of the Bull cult introduced nearly two thousand years earlier.

Index